CBT to Support Adults with ADHD

of related interest

OCD and Autism
A Clinician's Guide to Adapting CBT
Ailsa Russell, Amita Jassi and Kate Johnston
Illustrated by David Russell
ISBN 978 1 78592 379 1
eISBN 978 1 78450 728 2

Helping Autistic Teens to Manage their Anxiety: Strategies
and Worksheets using CBT, DBT, and ACT Skills
Dr Theresa Kidd
ISBN 978 1 78775 450 8
eISBN 978 1 80501 578 9

Challenging OCD in Young People with ASD
A CBT Manual for Therapists
Amita Jassi
Illustrated by Lisa Jo Robinson
ISBN 978 1 78775 288 7
eISBN 978 1 78775 289 4

CBT to Support Adults with ADHD

A THERAPIST'S GUIDE

**Antonia Dittner,
Trudie Chalder,
Katharine Rimes** and
Ailsa Russell

Jessica Kingsley Publishers
London and Philadelphia

First published in Great Britain in 2026 by Jessica Kingsley Publishers
An imprint of John Murray Press

2

A CIP catalogue record for this title is available from the
British Library and the Library of Congress

ISBN 978 1 80501 764 6
eISBN 978 1 80501 765 3

Printed and bound in the United States by Integrated Books International

Jessica Kingsley Publishers' policy is to use papers that are natural, renewable
and recyclable products and made from wood grown in sustainable
forests. The logging and manufacturing processes are expected to conform
to the environmental regulations of the country of origin.

Jessica Kingsley Publishers
Carmelite House
50 Victoria Embankment
London EC4Y 0DZ

www.jkp.com

John Murray Press
Part of Hodder & Stoughton Ltd
An Hachette Company

The authorised representative in the EEA is Hachette Ireland,
8 Castlecourt Centre, Dublin 15, D15 XTP3, Ireland (email: info@hbgi.ie)

Contents

Contents

Acknowledgements

Evaluation of the therapy and development of this book has taken many years, and numerous people have contributed. We would like to thank our colleagues both past and present at South London and Maudsley NHS Trust. There are too many to mention but we particularly wish to thank Declan Murphy and Martin Anson for early ideas on research design and Marie Sjoedin for trial therapy and contributions to earlier versions of the trial manual on which this book is based, as well as Abigail Oliver, Elizabeth Leahy, Inga Boellinghaus, Sophie Doswell and Hannah Winfield for invaluable feedback on the book and the handouts. Beyond the Trust, enormous thanks to Tom Gardner and Liz Dittner for comments and support in preparing the manuscript.

We also wish to acknowledge that the therapy described builds on the work of many dedicated and groundbreaking psychological researchers, theorists and practitioners including David Barlow, Aaron T. Beck, Judith Beck, Dennis Greenberger, Melanie Fennell and Marsha Linehan. We refer you to their excellent books (see References) for more comprehensive explanations of their ideas. We also acknowledge the psychological work on adult ADHD by Jessica Bramham, Russell Ramsay, Steven Safren and Susan Young that has helped shape our thinking.

We would like to thank South London and Maudsley NHS Trust for the space and time to develop and evaluate this therapy and the Biomedical Research Council for funding in the early stages.

Finally, and above all, we would like to express our gratitude to all the clients we have had the pleasure to work with over the years, who have been willing to share their time, experiences and insights and whose feedback has helped develop this approach. We learn so much from each person we work with and strive to continually refine our intervention approaches. This work would not have been possible without them, and we hope it will benefit many others.

Introduction

Adult Attention Deficit Hyperactivity Disorder (ADHD) profoundly affects day-to-day life and causes significant emotional distress. While increasing numbers of people are diagnosed with adult ADHD, and seek care from mental health services, therapists report they lack confidence and knowledge of how best to support them. The unfortunate result is that many people with adult ADHD cannot access psychological support.

There is growing evidence that cognitive behavioural therapy (CBT) helps manage both the core symptoms of ADHD and the associated emotional impact. It is one of the key recommended management approaches in the NICE guidelines for adult ADHD (National Institute for Health and Care Excellence, 2018).

This book aims to help therapists deliver evidence-based CBT for adults with ADHD. It is adapted from a therapist manual developed during a randomized controlled trial carried out in our national specialist NHS service at the Maudsley Hospital (Dittner *et al.*, 2018). We aim to present the approach used in a clear, step-by-step manner. We show you how to work with the client to formulate, develop and deliver an individually tailored CBT intervention.

Individual experiences of adult ADHD vary widely so there is no 'one size fits all'. As we will show, one of the advantages of a formulation-driven approach is that it enables the therapist to tailor the content of an intervention to each person, directly targeting the specific problems, beliefs and behaviours in each case, so enhancing both the therapeutic alliance and therapy outcomes. We will describe how to formulate and plan this therapy, offering a range of techniques that can be selected as indicated by the formulation and by the client's needs and goals.

The process of assessment and co-developing the formulation also lets us consider the impact of growing up with neurodevelopmental differences. In many cases, these differences have been misunderstood or unsupported, leaving the client at a disadvantage compared with their peers. Clients may have experienced overt criticism or discrimination. Such experiences can lead to negative self-beliefs and coping behaviours (such as procrastination) that, while understandable, may inadvertently worsen challenges and associated distress. Understanding these factors can help the client develop self-compassion and recognize how difficult experiences came about. They can start to see themselves, others and the world in a new light and find new ways of responding to their challenges.

We refer in this book to the clinical diagnosis of adult ADHD, as this is integral to the health services context in which we work, and the therapeutic approach we set out was developed to support people meeting a clinical threshold, i.e. experiencing significant impairment and distress because of their ADHD. We do not suggest that all people with these characteristics require therapy or even a diagnosis if these are not meaningful or helpful for them. We instead take a neuro-affirmative approach: neurodevelopmental conditions such as ADHD are not pathologies that need to be fixed. *Differences* in cognition and in how people experience and interact with the world are *not deficits*. We aim to help people to understand, appreciate and celebrate their own unique range of strengths and needs. We help them recognize where they are already coping well, how to build on this and how to develop additional strategies or enlist further support to manage difficult tasks or situations.

HOW TO USE THIS BOOK

This book is intended for therapists already familiar with the fundamentals of cognitive behavioural conceptualization and therapy. It therefore assumes knowledge of standard CBT techniques such as activity scheduling, thought challenging and common emotion regulation strategies. It focuses on the ways you would use these techniques differently and on things to hold in mind when working with ADHD. It is written to provide concrete and practical guidance for therapists at all stages. We acknowledge that some suggestions may already be second nature to more experienced readers, while still helpful to include for others. It assumes knowledge of assessing suitability for CBT and case management needs, including assessing and managing risk.

This book also assumes a working knowledge of ADHD. It focuses on how to use a formulation-driven approach to tailor a CBT intervention to the client's needs. Chapter 12 suggests some additional resources that provide more about the condition, and additional skills or strategies to incorporate into your therapy plan. You will learn most from working alongside people with ADHD and being open and curious about their personal experience – do not be afraid to ask questions so that you can learn.

The approach described here has so far been evaluated only in people with an established diagnosis of adult ADHD. With this caveat, it may be helpful for those with some of the challenges of the condition still awaiting ADHD diagnostic assessment. A further caveat is that the trial excluded those with additional psychiatric diagnoses, including anxiety, depression and substance use. It also excluded those with diagnoses of other neurodevelopmental conditions such as autism, which we know co-occur frequently with ADHD. However, an additional advantage of the formulation-driven approach is that it allows for a transdiagnostic approach to assessment and therapy so that the ADHD and co-morbidities such as depression and anxiety and other neurodevelopmental conditions can be addressed concurrently.

Some of the techniques and ideas described in this book may therefore be integrated into the therapy plans for people where adult ADHD-related challenges are present but are not the primary focus of therapy. Nevertheless, we would encourage you to consider with the client whether additional significant mental health or neurodevelopmental conditions require other sorts of support as a priority over the ADHD, while making adaptations or reasonable adjustments for the ADHD (some of the adaptations described in Chapter 2 may be of help here). Consideration of risk and impact on functioning are likely to be key factors in this decision.

In Chapter 1 we first set out the background to formulation-driven CBT for adult ADHD and the reasons for using this approach. In Chapter 2 we then suggest ways to adapt CBT when working with clients with ADHD, including ways to scaffold therapy to make it more accessible and ways to engage and motivate clients. In subsequent chapters we present the main components of the therapy as it was delivered over 16 sessions in the randomized controlled trial. Chapter 3, 'Assessment and Therapy Planning', describes Stage 1 of the process which includes assessment, co-developing the formulation and agreeing therapy goals. We suggest you follow this section carefully to establish a good basis of engagement and understanding for the sections that follow. In Chapters 4–8 we describe Stage 2: Active Therapy, which takes place over sessions 4–13, and the main components of this stage. These components can be selected in any order, as indicated by the formulation and the client's needs and goals. In Chapter 9 we cover Stage 3: Ending Therapy and Looking Ahead, which takes place over sessions 14–16 and includes how to summarize therapy and prepare the client for more independent work to maintain their therapeutic gains once sessions are finished.

We then cover additional challenges and considerations in Chapter 10. In Chapter 11 we conclude by recapping the key elements of the process. Chapter 12 includes useful resources.

The Appendices include the client handouts that we developed and used in the trial. We have updated them using client and therapist feedback as we have developed our practice. It is not intended that you use all of these: there are core handouts that you may find helpful for most cases and supplementary ones that you can select in addition, depending on their relevance to each case. All handouts in Appendix 1 and 2 can be downloaded as PDFs from https://digitalhub.jkp.com/redeem using the code QLFCSKE.

We have included client vignettes in both the manual and the handouts. We based these on more than one person rather than any singular client to ensure anonymity, and no real names have been used.

The client handouts are designed as psychoeducation materials and to form a personalized record of the therapy process. We intend them to be used to support the therapy process but not for self-therapy. Some clients will be able to read and complete client sections of the handouts for homework, whilst others will need support in the sessions.

The handouts include sections for the client to make notes both for their own reference and to inform in-session discussions. There are worksheets and record forms (e.g. target record forms) to support homework tasks. We recommend that you encourage your client to complete them themselves and to take an active part in the process: they can annotate and use colour or highlight sections to aid information processing and memory. We ask the client to keep their completed handouts and record forms in one place (either electronically or as printed paper copies) so that they can refer to them once sessions have ended to maintain changes made in therapy.

This book aims to provide you with a framework and tools to co-develop unique formulations and therapy plans with your clients, to which you can bring your combined ideas and imaginations. We have found working with adults with ADHD to be endlessly creative and inspiring and are glad to share this with you here. We wish you all the best and hope you find it helpful.

CHAPTER 1

Formulation-Driven CBT for ADHD

THE IMPACT OF ADULT ADHD

Once thought to be a childhood condition, it is now recognized that ADHD affects adults too. Increasing numbers of adults have, or are seeking, a diagnosis of adult ADHD. Globally, prevalence in children is around 5% (Polanczyk *et al.*, 2014) whilst prevalence in adults is 2.6–6.8% (Song *et al.*, 2021).

ADHD is characterized by inattention, impulsivity and hyperactivity. There are three diagnostic subtypes: the inattentive subtype (20–30% of cases), the hyperactive-impulsivity subtype (about 15% of cases) and the combined subtype which features inattention, hyperactivity and impulsivity together (50–75% of cases).

In everyday life, inattention, hyperactivity and impulsivity can present as memory problems (forgetting meetings, appointments), disorganization (losing things, incurring debts), poor time management (missed deadlines, lack of planning), procrastination, novelty-seeking behaviour, mood instability and social relationship problems. There are also some commonly reported difficulties not completely captured by the diagnostic criteria such as trouble staying awake or alert in boring situations and slowed information processing.

ADHD has a significant impact on multiple aspects of life including education, employment, physical health, mental health and social relationships (Faraone *et al.*, 2015). It often occurs in the context of other psychiatric disorders; co-morbidity rates are more than 75% (Katzman *et al.*, 2017), most frequently mood and anxiety disorders, substance use disorders and personality disorders.

Considering these factors, and that in many cases ADHD challenges become apparent from early childhood, it is perhaps unsurprising that people with ADHD experience a significant impact on psychological functioning. There is also evidence that environmental factors such as parental mental health diagnoses are more common in people with ADHD (Björkenstam *et al.*, 2017). Exposure to these environmental factors and adverse life experiences can be cumulative, creating multiple risk factors for psychological distress.

The presentations and challenges of ADHD are heterogeneous – there is no 'typical' presentation, and one size does not fit all. In psychological services, however, the main areas of psychological distress associated with ADHD tend to be as follows:

Low self-esteem. This is characterized by negative self-beliefs around failure, incompetence, unreliability, being different or unacceptable. Clients often report negative experiences in relation to their ADHD challenges and behaviour, including being in an education system that did not meet their needs and punitive or rejecting reactions from others. There are often high levels of shame and self-criticism.

Relationship difficulties. Many people report challenges in social interactions in relation to their ADHD characteristics such as not taking turns in conversation, interrupting or being 'overly' emotional. They report negative feedback from others and, following this, both self-consciousness and marked sensitivity to rejection.

Low mood and depression. Adverse life events such as difficulties in completing schoolwork as a child and beliefs about not having achieved one's potential or falling short of expectations can lead to a sense of a lack of achievement or mastery and susceptibility to low mood or depression. Other contributory factors include experiences of social rejection and a lack of supportive relationships, and there may be guilt or regret over the consequences of impulsive actions or thoughts about letting others down.

Anxiety. Fear of failure and concerns about competence are common, leading to anticipatory anxiety, self-consciousness, worries about performance and avoidance (such as procrastination). Anxiety can exacerbate attentional and impulsivity difficulties, leading to further anxiety about the impact of core ADHD characteristics on performance, resulting in a vicious cycle.

Emotion regulation difficulties. These are reported by many to be a central challenge of their ADHD. Anger, frustration and irritability are common, as are intense feelings of sadness or distress, the latter often triggered by perceived failure or rejection. Emotional regulation challenges may contribute to feelings of overwhelm and 'sensory overload' (*hyper* arousal) as well as demotivation and fatigue (*hypo* arousal) and fluctuations between these hyper and hypo aroused states. Challenges in emotional regulation can exacerbate other ADHD challenges such as distractibility, again resulting in a vicious cycle.

Impacts of the diagnosis. These include experiences of stigma and feelings of grief, loss and anger, as well as dilemmas or uncertainties around whether to disclose their diagnosis.

TERMINOLOGY

Many people prefer terms that reflect 'identity first' (e.g. disabled person) rather than 'person first' (person with a disability). The National Autistic Society (NAS) guidance (n.d.), based on research with autistic people, is to use identity-first terminology when referring to autistic people. We acknowledge we are using person-first language throughout this book. This is because it is common terminology across healthcare settings and there is, as yet, no equivalent research on community preferences for ADHD. In the absence of such research, we consider it good practice to routinely ask our clients how they prefer to refer to ADHD in relation to themselves.

FRAMEWORKS FOR UNDERSTANDING ADHD

There are different frameworks, or 'lenses', to view ADHD that do not necessarily exclude each other. First, there is the *medical model* which views ADHD as a disorder or clinical diagnosis that can be helped by therapy. We use this when we refer to ADHD as a diagnostic construct and do so because it is part of the healthcare context in which we work. An advantage of referring to ADHD as a diagnosis is that it provides a tool for people to speak up for themselves, advocate for their needs and have their challenges and needs understood.

The *social model of disability* says that people are disabled by barriers in society rather than their differences. Seen through this lens, rather than seeking to 'fix' ADHD in the individual, we can think about how to remove those barriers to promote equity and inclusion, for example by providing support and accommodating differences.

Neurodiversity is a term coined by Australian sociologist Judy Singer in the late 1990s. The neurodiversity movement emerged from the disability and civil rights movements, responding to marginalization and discrimination. Neurodiversity is a framework for understanding the naturally occurring diversity in human brain function – no two brains are alike in how they process information and interact with the world around them. In the neurodiversity framework, differences are not deficits.

Neurodivergence is a term used to describe when an individual diverges from the expected societal or 'typical majority' brain function. Neurodivergence is an 'umbrella' term that includes neurodevelopmental conditions such as ADHD, autism and dyslexia but also intellectual disability, mental illness and neurological disease. It is important to acknowledge that neurodivergent conditions are often not neatly compartmentalized. People with ADHD frequently have a co-occurring neurodivergent condition such as autism or dyslexia, and they can have intellectual disability.

NEURO-AFFIRMATIVE APPROACH
We use a neuro-affirmative approach which can incorporate aspects of all these frameworks. Fundamentally, a neuro-affirmative approach is one in which we:

- recognize the ways in which people with ADHD think and interact with the world
- see these as differences not deficits
- recognize and support these differences without seeking to correct them
- understand that distress may result from barriers in the environment and therefore encourage an inclusive environment that values and supports differences.

GUIDELINES AND EVIDENCE FOR PSYCHOLOGICAL INTERVENTIONS FOR ADULT ADHD

Guidelines for the management of adult ADHD in the UK (National Institute for Health and Care Excellence, 2018) and internationally (e.g. Australia, Canada) recommend both pharmacological and non-pharmacological treatment and support. Medication is the recommended first-line treatment. While many people with ADHD find medication helpful, a significant number are not able to tolerate medication, do not respond to medication or do not reach optimal outcomes on medications alone (Shim *et al.*, 2016; Schein *et al.*, 2022). Furthermore, medications do not inherently provide helpful coping strategies or address negative thoughts and self-beliefs. CBT is one of the recommended non-pharmacological management approaches due to growing evidence showing its benefits. Studies with the best results tend to be short-term, highly structured programmes with an emphasis on teaching specific skills and strategies and encouraging practice outside of the session (Fullen *et al.*, 2020; Liu *et al.*, 2023).

BACKGROUND OF THE RESEARCH TRIAL OF INDIVIDUAL FORMULATION-DRIVEN CBT FOR ADULT ADHD

Several research studies investigate group treatments. Advantages of groups include their cost-effectiveness and the role of social support in sharing experiences, reducing shame and stigma. We have previously delivered group psychoeducation interventions for adult ADHD, and these benefits were clear – such interventions have an important role in psycho-social support for this condition. However, given the heterogeneity of the condition and the very different needs of people seeking support, a group approach could not easily address the clients' idiosyncratic experiences and challenges.

Furthermore, previous scientifically evaluated psychological approaches, including individualized therapies, were predominantly skills based (i.e. focused on developing new skills or psychological 'tools' to manage challenges). We were interested in the specific cognitions and behaviours that could worsen the challenges and distress associated with having ADHD and that had been described by other researchers (Ramsay and Rostain, 2014). Individual formulation-driven CBT approaches, that are already used for other common mental health problems such as depression (Beck *et al.*, 1979) but adapted for ADHD, enable therapists to target the specific cognitions and behaviours directly. Formulation helps clients discover how their challenges have developed and are maintained, leading to feeling understood and accepted, and empowering them to cope (Redhead, Johnstone and Nightingale, 2015). We hypothesized that an individual formulation-driven approach, emphasizing the context of ADHD, could increase therapy efficacy and address commonly co-occurring psychological distress.

We were using individual formulation-driven CBT for adults with ADHD in routine clinical practice with good preliminary results. We therefore carried out a proof-of-concept, randomized controlled trial to formally evaluate the intervention. The protocol and results of the study were published in peer-reviewed academic journals (Dittner *et al.*, 2014; Dittner *et al.*, 2018). We compared two groups – a group receiving CBT combined with 'treatment as usual' (referred to as the CBT group) and a group receiving treatment as usual only (the TAU group). Consistent with our initial hypotheses, those in the CBT group showed significantly greater improvements in both ADHD symptoms (self- and other-rated) and everyday occupational and social functioning. In addition, there were significant improvements in clinical global improvement, anxiety, depression, global distress and satisfaction in the CBT group compared with the TAU group.

This book is based on the manual developed for the trial and aims to share the key components of this efficacious therapy as it was delivered.

ADVANTAGES OF FORMULATION-DRIVEN CBT FOR ADHD

Formulation-driven CBT targets the idiosyncratic cognitions and behaviours associated with adult ADHD. ADHD is a lifelong developmental condition which has a wide-ranging effect on emotional, social and cognitive development. For example, children with ADHD often experience difficulties at school (e.g. attentional and behavioural problems) and may receive negative feedback from parents, teachers and peers. These experiences can lead to the formation of negative self-beliefs that persist into adulthood, similar to those in depression, anxiety and low self-esteem, along with the common unhelpful coping responses seen in those conditions (such as experiential avoidance, perfectionism, etc.). These beliefs and behaviours, in combination with the ongoing ADHD characteristics, can worsen challenges, impact on functioning and cause distress; emotional and behavioural challenges often extend beyond the core characteristics or symptoms.

When we discuss with someone a formulation of their difficulties, we develop a shared hypothesis about what contributes to and maintains challenges. In ADHD we consider:

1. the individual's predispositions (e.g. cognitive strengths and challenges, personality)
2. their experiences growing up with ADHD (e.g. negative feedback from others due to attentional or behavioural difficulties)
3. how, in combination, their predispositions and experiences have contributed to certain beliefs (core beliefs and rules for living) and unhelpful coping (compensatory strategies)
4. how beliefs and unhelpful coping lead to situation-specific thoughts, emotions, physical reactions and behavioural responses that...
5. maintain beliefs and...
6. worsen the ADHD-related challenges.

These are illustrated in Image 1.

Therapy is then tailored to the individual and focuses on idiosyncratic unhelpful behaviours and thoughts identified in the detailed assessment, drawing on a range of evidence-based strategies. A formulation-driven approach is structured with focus on specific skills and strategies (such as time management), but it also uses the assessment to identify the client's main challenges and associated beliefs and behaviours, making it possible to target them directly.

The formulation enables the client and therapist to collaboratively address the core challenges of ADHD using information (psychoeducation), adaptations to the client's environment (including putting in place appropriate support) and repetition of adaptive skills to compensate for executive functioning differences. At the same time, they can identify and address the thoughts (e.g. 'I cannot concentrate so there is no point trying') and behaviours (e.g. procrastination) that maintain challenges and distress.

The therapist can help the client explore links between their beliefs and pertinent early life experiences in a compassionate and understanding way which helps to address common feelings of shame. This tailored approach not only helps clients to manage challenges, but it also helps them understand triggers, maintaining factors and helpful/unhelpful coping responses, supporting them to learn tools to manage in the future. This approach makes it possible to address emotional distress such as anxiety, low mood and shame alongside the ADHD.

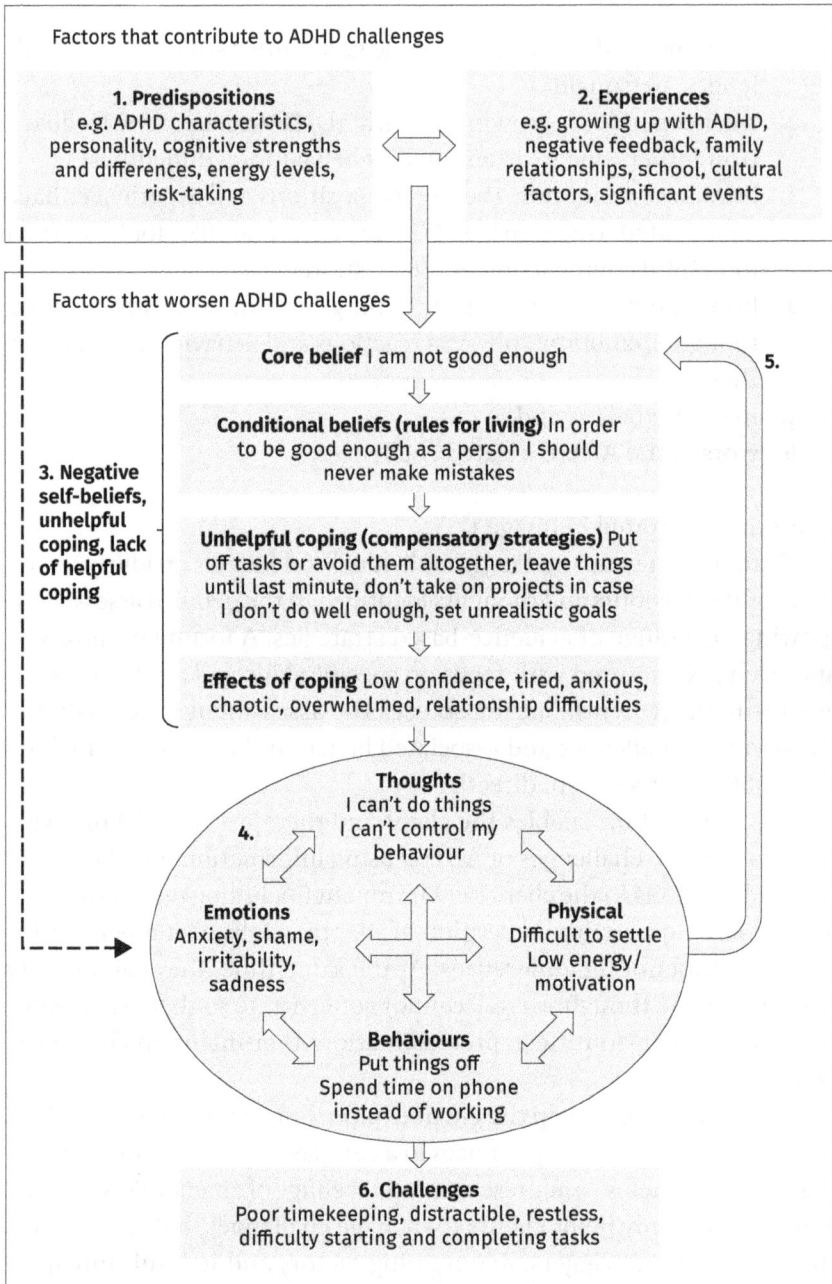

Factors that contribute to ADHD challenges

1. Predispositions
e.g. ADHD characteristics, personality, cognitive strengths and differences, energy levels, risk-taking

2. Experiences
e.g. growing up with ADHD, negative feedback, family relationships, school, cultural factors, significant events

Factors that worsen ADHD challenges

3. Negative self-beliefs, unhelpful coping, lack of helpful coping

Core belief I am not good enough

Conditional beliefs (rules for living) In order to be good enough as a person I should never make mistakes

Unhelpful coping (compensatory strategies) Put off tasks or avoid them altogether, leave things until last minute, don't take on projects in case I don't do well enough, set unrealistic goals

Effects of coping Low confidence, tired, anxious, chaotic, overwhelmed, relationship difficulties

Thoughts
I can't do things
I can't control my behaviour

Emotions
Anxiety, shame, irritability, sadness

Physical
Difficult to settle
Low energy/ motivation

Behaviours
Put things off
Spend time on phone instead of working

6. Challenges
Poor timekeeping, distractible, restless, difficulty starting and completing tasks

Image 1: An ADHD CBT formulation

OVERVIEW OF FORMULATION-DRIVEN CBT FOR ADHD

In our trial, therapy was delivered over 16 sessions. The first 15 sessions took place over 30 weeks. Sessions were one to two weeks apart, starting weekly where possible and moving to fortnightly sessions after a few weeks. There was a 16th 'follow-up' session at 42 weeks. The principle is to meet more frequently while embedding new habits and strategies and then to taper sessions towards the end of therapy to allow the client to become more independent and prepare for the end of therapy. In our experience of routine practice, there is some flexibility as to the number of sessions delivered, and it can be varied in response to client need.

Interventions were tailored to the individual, with therapists and clients deciding together what to cover and when, based on the formulation of the client's difficulties and their goals.

We therefore summarize the therapy components by therapy stage rather than session by session, as they vary depending on the individual therapy plan. These stages and their contents are summarized in Table 1 together with the session numbers, the chapters of the book that describe them and the corresponding handouts. They will be described in the following chapters.

A formulation-driven therapy plan will include the following components:

Thoughts and beliefs.
- Identifying and challenging negative automatic thoughts (NATs) and negative self-beliefs.
- Helping the client experiment with new beliefs and coping strategies.
- Developing new, positive self-beliefs, recognizing strengths, supporting self-actualization.

Behavioural support.
- Facilitating new executive functioning skills (e.g. managing attention).
- Helping the client establish helpful habits (e.g. daily routines).
- Identifying environmental support (home, work, etc.).

Emotional regulation.
- Providing information about emotions.

- Helping the client recognize the role of emotions in ADHD challenges.
- Helping them learn to respond to challenging emotional experiences in more helpful ways.

In the next chapter we will focus on general principles of adapting CBT to make it more accessible for adults with ADHD.

Table 1: A summary of the therapy stages, session numbers, chapters and handouts

Therapy stages and session numbers	Content	Chapter	Handouts
Stage 1 Assessment and Therapy Planning Sessions 1–3	• Assessment and psychoeducation • Socialize to CBT model • Develop initial formulation • Agree goals and start to work towards them	3	**Core Handout:** CBT and Adult ADHD
Stage 2 Active Therapy Sessions 4–13	• Day-to-day management of core challenges: scaffold and facilitate the acquisition of new skills and habits (e.g. time management, organization) • Identify environmental adaptations, support and reasonable adjustments • Develop behavioural strategies for managing main ADHD challenges	5	**Supplementary Handout:** Activity Diaries **Supplementary Handout:** Managing Distractions **Supplementary Handout:** Time Management
	• Identify and challenge negative automatic thoughts (NATs) that worsen ADHD challenges	6	**Core Handout:** Thinking Patterns in ADHD
	• Emotion regulation for managing impulsivity and procrastination, explore alternative responses to emotional experiences	7	**Core Handout:** Managing Emotions and Impulses **Supplementary Handout:** Procrastination **Supplementary Handout:** Anger
	• Address longer-term factors using a longitudinal formulation. Identify and modify underlying beliefs and compensatory behaviours that worsen ADHD challenges	8	**Core Handout:** Beliefs and Coping **Supplementary Handout:** Perfectionism

Stage 3 Ending Therapy and Looking Ahead Sessions 14 and 15	• Discuss and prepare for ending • Develop shared therapy summary document • Re-rate goals	9	**Core Handout:** Ending Therapy and Looking Ahead
Follow-up Session 16	• Review period since session 15 • Problem-solve and support the client to maintain changes made during active therapy • Re-rate goals		

Adapting CBT for Adult ADHD

Before embarking on assessment and therapy, it is helpful to consider how ADHD can impact on therapy and the sorts of adaptations that may be useful.

IMPACT OF ADHD ON THERAPY

People with ADHD may forget to attend sessions or attend late; they may be distractible, talk a lot or change topic. They may forget what has been talked about or find it hard to do homework tasks or to set realistic goals. ADHD challenges may have impacted on previous therapies, so clients may come with thoughts such as 'Therapy doesn't work for me' or 'I'm a hopeless case' that could affect their confidence or willingness to fully engage. Certain adaptations and considerations can make CBT more accessible for people with ADHD.

EXECUTIVE FUNCTIONING DIFFERENCES

Executive functioning is the term for 'higher-level' thinking skills that are essential for goal-directed behaviour and self-management. These include planning, sequencing, inhibition, working memory (holding information in mind while thinking about it), staying focused despite distractions and emotion regulation. The executive functions have been described as the 'control room' of the brain.

In ADHD there may be differences in one or more of the executive functions compared with the individual's general intellectual abilities (i.e. their verbal and non-verbal reasoning). The patterns of executive functioning differences vary between individuals (Rincón, Morales and

Sandoval, 2024). In practical terms, some people with ADHD, though not all, will need support with the essential components of a talking therapy. Therapists can help by 'scaffolding' the therapy to compensate for differences whilst supporting the client to learn new self-management skills.

There is a close relationship between executive functioning and mood, and it is helpful to share this information with clients. While executive functioning underpins emotion regulation, intense emotional states, low mood and anxiety can also *affect* executive functioning, worsening working memory, cognitive flexibility and the ability to withhold impulsive responses. This means that by addressing mood and emotional regulation directly in therapy (Chapter 7), clients may see improvements in other aspects of executive functioning such as attention and working memory. Also, if clients are anxious about their attentional 'performance' (in work or social situations), a negative feedback loop may develop whereby they become self-focused and their attention worsens, leading to further negative appraisals and more anxiety. We can help clients learn about and address these vicious cycles.

PRACTICAL WAYS TO 'SCAFFOLD' AND ADAPT THERAPY

- Discuss the 'how' as well as the 'what'.
- Provide clear verbal and written information.
- Co-create a client Therapy Record.
- Offer breaks.
- Offer support with missed sessions or late arrival.
- Structure sessions.
- Offer support with homework tasks.

It is helpful to consider from an early stage how the client's presenting challenges, including executive functioning differences, may impact on the therapy, and possible adaptations. Either before or at the assessment, the therapist can ask the client whether they know what adaptations they need. The therapist can suggest additional adaptations based on the clinical notes and their observations of the client's challenges. Here are some suggestions.

Discuss the 'how' as well as the 'what'

As CBT therapists, we are used to talking about what clients would like to do differently; with ADHD, we make sure to also talk about 'how' they are going to do them. As such, early CBT sessions for ADHD often have a behavioural and practical focus. More information on the behavioural approaches is provided in Chapter 5 and information on breaking goals down into steps in Chapter 3.

Provide clear verbal and written information

We have found the following communication adaptations helpful.

Before the sessions, clearly communicate the time and place for the appointment as well as instructions for how to get to the appointment or join the virtual session. Confirm spoken communications in writing.

During sessions, we suggest you support spoken information with short written summaries. We find it works best to co-create these in the session rather than afterwards. You can write on a whiteboard or on paper as you go and encourage the client to add their own notes and ideas, creating shared materials that they can take away. Diagrams and pictures, in colour where possible, help explain and record your conversations. This not only makes it easier for the client to concentrate and process the information during the session but will also form a useful memory aid later.

If there are information-processing differences, try to keep sentences short and deliver both written and spoken information in 'chunks' or manageable units. When speaking, it is helpful to allow extra time for clients to process the information, to think about what you have said and to respond. Frequent recaps allow you to check their understanding and your own. Let clients know that they can ask you to repeat things as many times as they need.

Co-create a client Therapy Record

Our trial predated the COVID-19 pandemic, so most sessions were face to face and we used paper handouts and worksheets. We asked the clients to use an A4 folder to keep them all in one place. Now, handouts can also be electronic, but we still find it helpful to talk about how they will store them, for example in a clearly labelled electronic folder.

As to whether to use electronic or paper worksheets, the system that works best for an individual, and that they will use, is the one that is best for them. If the client is unsure, we encourage them to experiment.

There is evidence that writing by hand, as opposed to typing, activates multiple sensory and motor areas, deepening neural connections and making it easier to retrieve the information later (Van der Weel and Van der Meer, 2024). Therefore, if there are difficulties (in memory or attention) when using electronic worksheets or other materials, we might suggest the client try using paper versions.

Offer breaks

It can help to offer breaks in sessions, with the opportunity to leave for a brief walk or stretch if needed. This can be planned in advance and added to the agenda, or you can just agree with the client that they let you know when they need a break. In our experience, most clients prefer not to plan breaks on the agenda and rarely take them, either at their own request or the therapist's suggestion. Nonetheless, they say they value having the option to do so if needed.

Offer support for missed sessions and late arrival

Challenges such as forgetfulness, disorganization and procrastination can lead to missed sessions or late arrival. It helps to pre-empt this by addressing it early – before the first appointment if possible. If the client thinks this is likely to be an issue, problem-solve it with them. Most services provide appointment reminders. You and the client may agree they need extra prompts. If their goal is to learn to remember appointments by themselves, you may agree together that you stop your additional reminders at a certain point as they learn to use their own strategies.

From our experience, people often arrive on time for the first one or two appointments but start to arrive later as sessions progress. If the client arrives late to a session, we suggest you address it immediately, no matter what had been planned for that session, to help prevent it interfering with therapy. It helps to address it with curiosity, being sensitive to the client's self-critical thoughts or anticipated criticism. Frame the discussion as an opportunity to better understand the challenges that led to seeking support in the first place: 'I understand this is something that you find hard, and I am here to help you. This is a great opportunity for us both to understand what is going on here.'

For some clients, it can help to explore the situation in detail, asking about all aspects of the journey. People with ADHD typically underestimate the time needed for the journey and envisage the 'best case scenario', forgetting to allow realistic time frames for all the stages and possible delays. They may also find it hard to pay attention to the time and the passage of time. This is sometimes referred to as 'time blindness'.

For example: The bus journey to the psychology service takes 30 minutes, so the client starts to leave home 30 minutes before the appointment time. This does not allow time to get to the bus stop, time for the bus to arrive, time to walk from the bus stop to the service or contingency time for unexpected events (e.g. delayed bus).

Questions to ask about each stage:

Allowing time to get ready to leave

- What do you need to do before leaving the house? (List each task and estimate times.)
- What do you need to bring (and where are those things)?
- What time do you need to get up (and go to bed the night before)?

The journey

- How often does the bus come? Is it ever late?
- Does the bus journey always take 30 minutes or sometimes longer?
- How long does it take from your house to get to the bus stop?

The appointment

- What would it be like if you arrived a few minutes early?

Once all the sticking points have been identified, they can be addressed, for instance by allowing extra time, adding prompts where needed (from a partner/family member or phone alarm) and trying new ways of doing things.

Formulating negative automatic thoughts (NATs), emotions and physical sensations helps identify maintaining factors and ways to intervene. For example, one client realized he thought being on time would be boring and this was leading him to avoid it. We explored the pros and cons of arriving on time versus avoiding the wait. He decided to try arriving 15 minutes early, listening to music on headphones while he waited. He realized he was able to start the session on time and in a calmer state. He came to see this as worthwhile since he enjoyed it more and this 'buffer' time reduced the possibility, and resultant stress, of arriving late.

Structure sessions

Collaborative agenda setting is an essential part of CBT. It is good practice to allocate times to agenda items and be explicit about deviations. For ADHD clients, it helps to write out the agenda and keep it visible during the session, for example on a whiteboard. It also helps to have a visible clock or timepiece. You can then refer to the agenda and the time to keep the session 'on track' and demonstrate the process of time management. Analogue clocks, i.e. those with a clockface, work better than digital for many since they visually represent the passage of time. However, some clients may struggle with analogue clocks – for example if they have dyslexia or if they find the ticking sound distracting.

It helps to agree how you will keep the session on track. You can ask for permission to interrupt or redirect: 'Part of having ADHD can be having lots of ideas or different things to talk about – if we agree an agenda and I notice we have gone off-topic, is it OK if I interrupt you?' Most ADHD clients want help with staying on-topic, so you can then agree a sign to use to interrupt such as pointing to the agenda on the whiteboard, putting up a hand or saying, 'Can I stop you?'

The client may also want or need to interrupt. Skilled session management involves pointing out when the conversation has diverged from the agenda and agreeing whether to amend that session's agenda or to carry over the new topic to the next session. You can observe together the process of interrupting or getting distracted: 'Let's look at the agenda – if we talk about this now, we will not have time to talk about... What would you prefer to do?' If the client wants to stay with the initial topic but is worried about forgetting what they want to say if they do not say it immediately, encourage them to experiment with writing it down and coming back to it later.

It is helpful to comment on the process in a 'non-judgemental' way. You can explain that the session is a safe place to observe, reflect and try out different ways of interacting. This externalizes tangents as ADHD challenges that can be understood and supported, thereby reducing the risk of activating self-critical thoughts and self-beliefs. You can also ask about negative (including self-critical) automatic thoughts, emotions, physical sensations and action urges that arise, and address them, either in the moment or by making a note to return to them later.

Offer support with homework tasks

Although with therapists we use the term 'homework', we ask clients what they prefer to call it, as many have had aversive experiences of homework at school. They may prefer another term such as 'between-session tasks'. The rationale is the same as in all CBT, that is, to practise and reinforce in 'real life' the skills learned in the session and test out new thoughts, beliefs and behaviours.

Allow time both to set up the task(s) and to review in the next session. Set an expectation that they attempt it and that you ask about it in the next session. At the same time, pre-empt that they may not do it. You can frame it as a 'win-win': 'If you manage to do it, then it will be great that you have done it; however, if you don't, we will have useful information about what made it difficult.' Demonstrate understanding: 'Of course this is hard; you wouldn't be here if it wasn't – my job is to help you.' It helps to scaffold it as much as possible, thinking through in advance any barriers or challenges and identifying solutions such as asking a partner or family member to prompt or do it alongside.

There are record forms in Appendix 2; however, you and the client may decide between you to use other methods. For example, one client decided to organize his office by doing a little every day and to record this using a time-lapse video which he then played in the next session.

When a client comes to the session without having done agreed homework, it helps to explore this with curiosity and remind them you had both anticipated this. This is to minimize the possibility of activating self-critical thoughts. Again, it helps to frame it as an opportunity to understand what happened (or did not). We suggest you allow plenty of time for this in the session to find out what got in the way and identify possible solutions.

For example:

- If they forgot about it, schedule it for the following week but this time consider with them what could help – maybe an alarm or help from a partner or family member.
- If they remembered they needed to do it but put it off, explore the thoughts, feelings, physical sensations and behaviours associated with this. See Chapters 6 and 7 for ideas about how to address these.

It may help to revisit why you both agreed the tasks in the first place and how these relate to the therapy goal.

It is very important to praise (provide positive reinforcement – see Chapter 5) whatever the client comes back with, including partial completion. Acknowledge any steps towards doing the task(s) – for example: 'So you thought about it at least a couple of times in the week even if it wasn't possible to do it – that's great, bringing it to mind between sessions is the first step towards finding a time to do it – let's build on that!' Help them to identify and address any self-critical thoughts – for example, even if they have completed it, clients may apologize for their spelling or the presentation or may express annoyance with themselves for having put it off, in which case the associated self-critical thoughts can be discussed.

ENGAGEMENT

As with CBT for other conditions, essential aspects of engagement include co-constructing the formulation, introducing the CBT process and instilling hope. The formulation provides a framework to explain not only how difficulties developed but also how they have then been maintained. The formulation points to clear solutions, that is, it shows the client how changes in thinking and behaviour can help them approach challenges differently, so improving functioning and increasing self-efficacy. People with ADHD very often report at this early stage that they find the structure, diagrams and discussion of practical solutions encouraging, counteracting feelings of confusion, overwhelm and hopelessness.

As you co-construct the formulation, you will identify links between their experiences growing up with a neurodevelopmental condition, possible early behavioural difficulties and the beliefs they have developed about themselves and others. For example, it is understandable that someone who struggles to complete tasks could have concluded that they are 'lazy', and that others are critical of them if they have experienced negative feedback or experienced difficulties compared with their peers. It makes sense that someone would learn to cope by avoiding tasks if they were not supported to learn the requisite skills for approaching and completing tasks or were criticized for their efforts. You can identify and provide information about vicious cycles between executive functioning differences and mood. Experiences take on a different meaning (are 're-framed') when considered in the context of having a differing learning style that was perhaps not recognized or accommodated. You can also highlight strengths, resilience and helpful coping strategies, pointing out what they have managed to do despite challenges and all the efforts they have made.

Compassion

Re-evaluating experiences in this way helps the client view challenges more compassionately. As we have seen, for understandable reasons given the lifelong nature of their challenges and the experiences of stigma, perceived 'failure' and negative feedback, there are often high levels of shame and self-criticism. Therefore, we feel it is particularly important with this client group for therapists to convey warmth and empathy actively and explicitly from the outset, although warmth and empathy are fundamental non-specific factors of any therapeutic interaction and a core competency for CBT (Blackburn et al., 2001). Drawing on ideas from Compassion Focused Therapy (Gilbert, 2010), we explain that being compassionate to ourselves is the first step to learning about how our minds work and how to manage them. Therapist compassion and validation of the difficult emotions and experiences (e.g. 'You didn't choose this' and 'You're doing the best you can') will help foster self-compassion in the client.

MOTIVATION
Expectations of change

During Stage 1: Assessment and Therapy Planning, elicit and address the client's expectations of change. It is important to say that no approach will be helpful all the time and that although therapy may help, it does not work for everyone. It does not usually make challenges or difficulties go away completely, and indeed, that is not the aim. Instead, we are helping people understand challenges and difficulties, view them differently, develop a more accepting attitude and, where appropriate, find ways to adapt to them or seek adaptations from others so they cause less distress.

Doubts and ambivalence

If clients express doubts or ambivalence, reflect this, empathize with their thoughts and emotions and explore them further (rather than engaging in debate or persuading). It is understandable, for example, if they have had difficult experiences with previous therapies that they would have doubts about this one. There may also be fears of 'failing' at therapy resulting from previous experiences that they consider to be failures, for example at school.

Some clients feel ambivalent about learning new skills or habits because they seem boring. They think they reduce opportunities for fun or spontaneous behaviour or perceive them as something that they 'should' or 'have to' do and therefore to be resisted – one client said, 'It is awful to be scheduled. I don't want to have to do it.' Simply reflecting this ambivalence can be helpful: 'On the one hand, you feel out of control, but on the other, you think using lists and structuring your time would be "awful".'

They may have beliefs about experiencing uncomfortable feelings, such as that they will not be able 'to stand' the boredom or discomfort associated with certain tasks. You can ask about the effects of these beliefs and explore the advantages and disadvantages of change. Encourage a spirit of curiosity and experimentation – it may or may not be helpful for them, but why not try it and see? Could they 'dip a toe' into difficult experiences? The client who thought structuring his time would be awful commented a few sessions later that: 'I have come to the conclusion that I do need a list. I can't remember to do everything and that leads to pressure.'

We suggest that information about practical skills only be provided in the context of working towards the client's own goals. We always ask permission before providing any further information or suggestions and then elicit the client's thoughts and emotions about them. It is helpful to frame them as experiments – 'Why not try it and see?' – rather than changes they 'should' be making.

Managing setbacks

Anticipate setbacks and frame them as a key part of the process so that the client is prepared for them. It helps to normalize slip-ups: we are all human and we all make mistakes and struggle at times. Learning to work towards goals is as much about how we respond when we do not stay 'on task' as it is about learning to carry out the plan. We know there are likely to be self-critical thoughts in ADHD. We can therefore encourage clients to observe such thoughts when they arise and instead try to respond with understanding and compassion. This will reduce distress and make it easier to get back on track more quickly. Addressing self-criticism is discussed further in Chapter 8.

Attending CBT is a significant commitment. It requires considerable time for both the sessions themselves and the homework over an extended period. It needs to be fitted around work, family and other obligations, and it takes courage to explore potentially distressing life events and challenges. Your acknowledgement of this will help them persevere: 'It is interesting that you believe you are lazy when I can see how hard you are working to understand yourself and make things better.'

GOALS
Making them relevant

As we have discussed, behavioural change is a key component of CBT for ADHD. Thus, goals are central to the process and can be a powerful motivator if set in collaboration with the client and used thoughtfully.

First, it is important that therapy goals feel personally relevant. As in any CBT, be sure to explore the reason for setting each goal and to whom it is most important. The client may have received the message from others that they need to do things a certain way, for example manage their time differently, but unless it feels meaningful for them, this will not motivate them to work towards that goal, especially if they perceive that it conflicts with other goals or values, such as the freedom to be spontaneous in their daily life. For this reason, there are no set 'modules' in formulation-driven CBT for ADHD – the goals are set in accordance with the client's own needs and wishes and informed by the formulation. It is also important to have regular therapy reviews to ensure that the goals remain relevant.

As neuro-affirming therapists, we understand that neurodivergent people often face challenges because of societal structures, not because there is something 'wrong' with them. So, in setting goals, we want to consider not only what changes can be made but also who can make them, that is, is it the individual or the organizations they are part of? We also think about reasonable adjustments in education or the workplace to help them access these and to advocate for themselves (see Chapter 10).

At the same time, to support the client within existing systems, we explore and work towards what *they* can do. They may hold self-limiting beliefs about their abilities that are outdated or have not been put to the test (e.g. 'It's better not to try than to fail'). We therefore support them to notice these as beliefs rather than facts, be curious and find out what is possible rather than to take at 'face value' assumptions that ADHD makes it impossible.

Keep it simple

Watch out for perfectionism when setting goals. We have observed that ADHD clients often have very high expectations for themselves. At the same time, they can find it hard to identify and work through the necessary steps to reach their goals, resulting in frustration and distress (see Chapter 10 and **Supplementary Handout:** Perfectionism). Clients will come to the first sessions with lots of ideas, hopes and expectations and the therapist can feel under pressure to address all of these at once.

We try to model a steady, realistic and methodical approach and to keep things simple. We know that executive functioning differences can affect information processing. Agreeing some simple concrete goals and working towards these early on will provide some quick 'wins'. We encourage the client to choose a couple at first and explain that we are working towards the principle of setting achievable goals. It may not be possible to do everything during therapy, but they will be learning strategies that they can apply to other goals later.

Chapter 2 summary

- ADHD can impact on therapy. We can scaffold therapy to support executive functioning differences and increase access.
- The co-constructed formulation provides a framework for understanding factors that contribute to and worsen ADHD challenges. This helps the client view their challenges more compassionately.
- Addressing clients' expectations of change, doubts and ambivalence and anticipating setbacks can help with motivation.
- Goals are central to CBT. It is key to make them collaborative, personally relevant, simple and realistic.

Assessment and Therapy Planning

STAGE 1: ASSESSMENT AND THERAPY PLANNING

The overall aims of Stage 1: Assessment and Therapy Planning are to start to form a therapeutic alliance, to help make sense of the client's experiences and challenges and to instil hope. Developing a shared formulation that considers the experience of growing up with ADHD is a central part of the engagement process. As you both reflect on the experiences, you build a shared understanding of the ADHD challenges, related difficulties (e.g. low self-esteem, anxiety), the ways in which these have developed and their impact.

This stage often takes place over three sessions.

Handout:

- **Core Handout**: CBT and Adult ADHD

SESSION 1 ASSESSMENT

It can be helpful to allow more time for the first session, that is, 60–90 minutes, to include a cognitive behavioural assessment, a summary and sharing the rationale for CBT for ADHD. It follows the same format as a standard CBT assessment (Beck, 2020); we provide a summary of the main assessment topics in the following box.

Session 1
60–90 minutes

1. Introductions, 'housekeeping', ask about preferred language and any reasonable adjustments required in the session. Briefly check knowledge of ADHD and explain the purpose of the session.

2. Assessment:

   a. What are the main challenges? Ask for one or more recent examples. For these examples, identify associated negative automatic thoughts (NATs), emotions, physical reactions and behaviours:

   Cognitive: NATs, E.g. 'What goes through your mind?' – listen for self-criticism and hopeless thoughts, and ask about thinking processes such as rumination and worry.
   Physical: E.g. wanting to move or fidget, tiredness or slowness, nausea, muscle tension.
   Emotional: E.g. sad, anxious, irritable, guilty, ashamed – how able are they to recognize, label and regulate their emotions?
   Behavioural: What do you do/not do?

   What was happening, when and where? What were the triggers, what made it better or worse, what happened afterwards?
   Start to build a cross-sectional ABC model.[1]

   b. Development of the challenge(s) and relevant personal history:

   • History of the development of the challenges.

---

[1]   ABC is an acronym for Antecedents (situations or activating events), Behaviour, Consequences. It is used as an assessment and formulation tool. When including cognitive factors in the assessment and formulation, it can be helpful to broaden the 'B' to 'Being' as a way of capturing everything that is happening in the moment – including thoughts going through an individual's head, what is happening in terms of bodily feelings, beliefs and emotions.

- Times when they were better/worse – what was going on at those times?
- When was the diagnosis (recent, in adulthood or childhood)? What does ADHD mean to them? What thoughts and feelings do they have about it (stigma, relief, anger, loss)?
- Significant others' attitudes and responses to their challenges (understanding, accommodating, critical, dismissive)?
- Family experiences – what were their parents like? Are other family members neurodivergent?
- Cultural factors – how is ADHD considered within the client's community?
- What made them seek help now?

c. Impact of challenges – home, work/study, self, relationships. Are they engaging in unhelpful coping such as perfectionism, hiding ADHD symptoms (masking) or procrastination?

d. Attempts to solve problems and address challenges including past psychological therapy, learned coping. Ask about strengths (or advantages of ADHD) and helpful coping strategies (even if since lapsed). Are they taking medication? What effect does this have? Do they take it as prescribed?

e. Description of a typical day – sleep, activity, rest, structure (or lack of structure).

f. Mood – current and past, co-morbidities, including traits or diagnoses of additional neurodevelopmental conditions such as autism.

3. Summarize and share initial formulation.

4. Describe the principles of CBT and rationale for therapy using their examples.

5. Set initial broad goals.

6. Discuss expectations for therapy (client and therapist), any possible difficulties (e.g. timekeeping) and how they can be overcome.

7. Ask for feedback, discuss questions or doubts.

8. Homework: **Core Handout:** CBT and Adult ADHD. Discuss storage of handouts and session notes.

We are aiming to find answers to the following questions:

- What are the main challenges?
- How did they develop and how are they maintained?
- What unhelpful thoughts and beliefs are associated with the problems; what reactions (emotional, physical and behavioural) are associated with this thinking?

We hypothesize:

- how the client's predisposition (e.g. cognitive strengths and challenges, personality characteristics) and experiences (including growing up with ADHD) have contributed to current challenges
- how the client has come to think about themselves, other people and the world; what underlying beliefs and associated coping behaviours have developed
- how beliefs and coping responses have given rise to situation-specific thoughts, emotions, physical reactions and behaviours
- what stressors, including growing up with ADHD (whether diagnosed or not), contributed to the development of the challenges and impacted on the client's coping or ability to address the challenges
- what advantages ADHD confers (e.g. hyperfocus, creativity, etc.) and what protective factors are present.

We will use a case example about Ali to illustrate the assessment. A fuller description of Ali can be found in **Core Handout**: CBT and Adult ADHD, along with an example of an initial formulation such as you would be developing with a client in Stage 1 of therapy. As the therapist, you will find it helpful to read this handout.

Case example: Ali

Ali is a 20-year-old man. He is an apprentice in a manufacturing company. His job is practical, and he is doing a college course which involves written assignments. His main challenges are in organization, starting and completing college assignments and getting into debt from impulsive spending.

As with any CBT, we begin the session with introductions and any 'housekeeping'. If you have not already done so, ask what adaptations they need, providing suggestions if necessary, and ask whether they have preferred language or terminology in relation to their ADHD. Agree ways to keep the session 'on-topic' (see Chapter 2 for more information).

We check the client's understanding and knowledge of ADHD and provide brief information about the main characteristics and common challenges of the condition as needed. We then ask for a description of their main challenges in relation to their ADHD, such as being disorganized, procrastinating or behaving impulsively.

We then explore the cognitive, emotional, physical and behavioural components of these. See the diagram below for some of Ali's examples. We start by constructing a cross-sectional model for one or more of the examples. We consider the situation or trigger (A), the thoughts, emotions, physical reactions and behaviours (B) and then the consequences (C). We suggest you include at least one thought or behaviour at B; it does not have to include all the elements shown below. You do not have to draw it if this will take too long, though it can help to do so. Often people find it hard to identify the thought or the emotions and find it easier to name physical reactions and behaviours.

Examples of Ali's ABCs:

(A) Situation		(B) Thoughts, emotions, physical reactions, behaviour		(C) Consequences

Situation: Get home from work, read message from friend asking him to game	⇨	**Thought:** I deserve to have fun **Behaviour:** Ignore college work, game with friend	⇨	**Consequence:** Think I can't control myself Feel anxious and frustrated
Situation: College assignment is due	⇨	**Thought:** I can't do it I'm never going to be able to do this **Emotion:** Nervous, anxious **Physical:** Can't settle, feel energetic **Behaviour:** Put off working, go on long cycle ride	⇨	**Consequence:** Assignment not done Don't feel confident, put it off more Don't want to go to college
Situation: See a new bike I want	⇨	**Thought:** It's got electronic shifting – it's professional level! **Emotions:** Excited **Physical:** Heart beats faster **Behaviour:** Buy bike	⇨	**Consequence:** Think I can't afford it I can't control myself I shouldn't have bought it Feel regretful and anxious

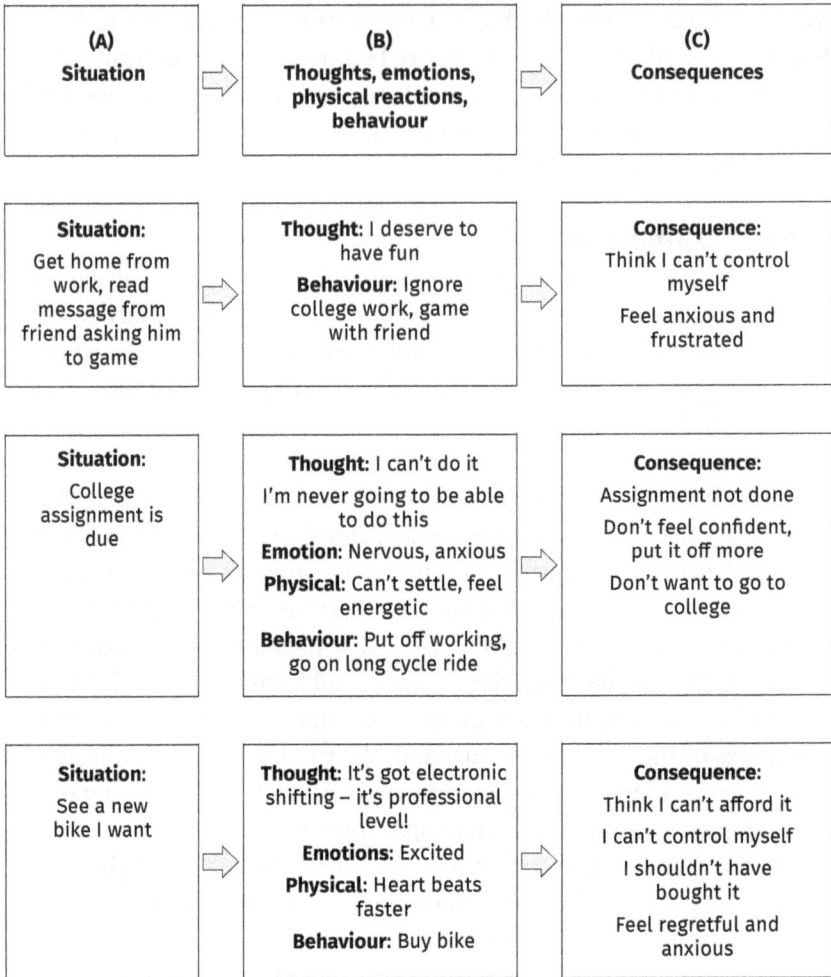

Later, in Stage 2: Active Therapy, we will look at the consequences in greater detail, as well as the ways in which these can maintain unhelpful thoughts and coping behaviours. Ask about the development of the challenges, personal and family history, mood and past psychological therapies. Use this information to form a preliminary longitudinal formulation. If possible, share this briefly at the end of the session – you will return to this in the following session in more detail.

We then explain that challenges are a result of the interaction between an individual's predisposition and their experiences. These give rise to ways of thinking that affect how we feel and what we do. Here is an example:

Therapist: So, Ali, you have said that you have had lifelong problems with concentration. You had some difficulties at school, were told off and you compared yourself to schoolfriends who found things easier. Does that reflect your experience?

Ali: Yes, that's it.

Therapist: How do you think that affects you now when you try and work?

Ali: I think, 'I can't do this', and I just want to do something else.

Therapist: So the thoughts lead you to want to do something else, to avoid...

Ali: Yes, and I just can't concentrate.

Therapist: So, it sounds like the concentration problems are still there and you have negative thoughts about your ability: 'I can't do this'...

Ali: Yes, that's it and, 'I'm never going to be able to do this.'

Therapist: I'm never going to be able to do this. Do you notice how it makes you feel?

Ali: I just want to do something else; I can't settle to it.

Therapist: You want to do something else; you can't settle – do you feel anything else in your body?

Ali: Just that I don't want to sit down and work. I want to move – I'm full of energy, I suppose.

Therapist: Are you aware of any emotions?

Ali: Is nervous an emotion? Uneasy...

Therapist: Anxious maybe?

Ali: Yeah, I guess that's it, I probably do feel a bit anxious; I hadn't thought about that before. I definitely feel anxious when I haven't done it...

Therapist: So, you think, 'I can't do it', you can't settle, there is some nervousness, possibly anxiousness – anxiety – you find it hard to concentrate and you want to do something else... What happens then?

Ali: Well, I put it off – this is one of my main problems – I just don't get things done. It's causing a lot of problems at college. I don't feel confident that I can do it.

Therapist: It's affecting your confidence...

Ali: Yeah, and because I don't feel confident, I put it off even more. Then I think, 'I'm never going to be able to do this' – sometimes I don't even want to go to college because it makes me think about all the things I'm struggling with. I would just rather not go. But I know that just makes it worse.

Therapist: So you feel even less like doing it – it sounds like a negative cycle.

We then explain how CBT can provide support, for example: 'CBT can help you recognize and break these cycles: by understanding more about your thoughts and coping behaviours, you can learn to respond differently so the ADHD challenges feel more manageable. Together we can find out what extra support you may need to help with that.'

It may then help to illustrate some ways that CBT may address some of the challenges that the client has raised. For example, for Ali this would be by helping him learn practical skills to manage concentration and helping him to notice and address negative thoughts ('I can't do it') and his avoidant coping.

We then provide an overview of key aspects of CBT such as collaboration, agendas and homework. We find it helpful to explain that we may offer reflections or observations of the client's thoughts and behaviours, both in general and in relation to the therapeutic process, and we ask permission to do so. You can use **Core Handout**: CBT and Adult ADHD to support this conversation. The handout contains information about adult ADHD, the CBT approach, what to expect from therapy, setting goals and writing a list of rewarding/pleasant activities. You can ask the client to read it for homework or read it with them in the session. Suggest that you will complete their own formulation and agree goals together over the next two sessions and that they can note down any ideas in the meantime.

Session 1 homework: **Core Handout**: CBT and Adult ADHD. Agree tasks related to storage of handouts and session notes; for example, find a notebook or A4 ring binder, create an electronic folder.

All following sessions are 50 minutes and follow a standard CBT structure (Beck, 2020).

Standard CBT session structure
50 minutes

- Brief update and check on mood.
- Bridge from previous session.
- Set agenda.
- Review homework.
- Discuss issues on the agenda.
- Set new homework.
- Summary and feedback.

SESSION 2

As with standard CBT, we start by asking the client how they found the previous session and check understanding and recollection. This provides opportunities for feedback and for addressing any misconceptions or concerns. If the assessment was not fully completed or if the client has thought of more relevant information since the previous session, we discuss this too.

We review the homework, that is, reading the handout and deciding how to store their Therapy Record. If the homework has not been completed, we discuss this in a curious and non-judgemental way (see Chapter 2). If needed, we engage in problem-solving with the client to help them with the homework or any other difficulties that may be arising, for example getting to the appointment on time.

We review **Core Handout**: CBT and Adult ADHD, ask whether there are any questions and provide further explanations where necessary. We check their understanding of the CBT approach and rationale for therapy and ask for reflections on the vignette, which provides an example of how a formulation is developed from the assessment information.

We complete the blank formulation in the handout using the client's own examples. This may have already been covered briefly in the previous session. If so, this is an opportunity to elaborate and reflect further. Where appropriate, we ask more about early life events and then explicitly link these to the development and maintenance of current challenges. For example, Ali's experiences of finding it hard to concentrate at school had led to negative thoughts and beliefs about his ability that are activated when he has college assignments to do.

The initial formulation is a simplification of the longitudinal model (see Chapter 1) and intended to be used to socialize to the CBT model. It just has spaces for predispositions and experiences, and how these have combined to give rise to thoughts/beliefs, physical sensations, emotions and behavioural responses, resulting in challenges. A more in-depth formulation is developed with the client later in therapy when the nature of core beliefs, conditional beliefs and coping behaviours (compensatory strategies) are explored further.

Clients often come to CBT with a biological understanding of their ADHD ('there is something wrong with my brain'). We aim to broaden this understanding to a bio-psycho-social perspective. Here, clients start to see how ADHD characteristics (in this case, hyperactivity) can fluctuate in relation to different situations, and the thoughts, emotions, physical sensations and behaviours that are activated. For example, Ali noticed that when he was anxious, he wanted to move and felt full of energy. A bio-psycho-social model helps people recognize that altering their thinking and behaviour could help with their challenges and that change is possible. It may shift the locus of control from external to internal, helping clients see that they can gain control. This is important since clients frequently report thoughts about being out of control or unreliable.

We also ask the client about any strengths or advantages of ADHD. For example, they may value being adventurous, curious or creative or their ability to 'hyperfocus'. Every characteristic can have advantages and disadvantages, and this usually depends on both the context and how it is perceived. Part of responding helpfully to ADHD is recognizing one's unique profile of strengths and challenges and learning to accept – and hopefully in due course to *celebrate* – the ADHD brain while learning to cope effectively with challenges and think about them in new ways.

Session 2 homework: Therapy goals are described in **Core Handout**: CBT and Adult ADHD. This will be used in the next session to discuss their goals. In the meantime, we invite them to think about their ideas for therapy goals. They may want to write something down, but they may choose not to. We suggest that we will complete Worksheet: Identifying Therapy Goals in **Core Handout**: CBT and Adult ADHD together at the next session.

SESSION 3
We review the client's understanding of the formulation and their experience of the process, eliciting thoughts and/or reactions and addressing any misunderstandings.

Setting goals
It helps to revisit the rationale, explaining that setting goals is a central component of CBT for all conditions, providing direction and focus for the behavioural changes. Furthermore, setting realistic goals and identifying the incremental steps needed to reach them is a common challenge for many people with ADHD. In therapy, clients can be supported to develop skills that they can apply in other settings.

While goals are action focused, the point is not to make the client more 'productive'; indeed, if the client is overworking, the goals may help them identify a manageable balance between work and other important areas of life, which may mean working *less*. The goals are a tool to help think about practical changes that are valuable and meaningful to the client.

Help the client to set SMART (specific, measurable, achievable, realistic and timebound) goals. You can use the visual scales in **Core Handout**: CBT and Adult ADHD to record these. In our trial, we asked clients to identify *up to* four goals. These will ideally be related to the main ADHD challenges that they have already described and will be different for each person.

We will use a case example about Yemi to illustrate setting goals here and in the handout.

Case example: Yemi

Yemi is a 41-year-old woman. She is a lawyer and works three days per week, looking after her young children on the other days. Her main challenges are feeling overwhelmed and chaotic, procrastination and anger outbursts.

Yemi's goals
Procrastination:

- To complete all reports the day before the deadline.

Planning:

- To leave the house on time in the morning.

Anger:

- To hold myself back from snapping at my husband.

Make time for myself:

- To go to an exercise class every Saturday.

Yemi's first goal was around procrastination; she was working late into the evening when deadlines were due and said that instead she would like to aim to complete them the day before the deadline. Yemi needed help to 'operationalize' some of her challenges – for example, she said,

'I would like to feel less overwhelmed.' Rather than having a goal about a feeling, it is helpful to identify specific concrete goals by asking questions such as, 'If you were less overwhelmed, what would you be doing differently/more of/less of?' Alternatively say, 'Tell me about a recent situation when you felt overwhelmed', and from there, explore what led to that feeling.

Yemi realized that she felt overwhelmed when trying to leave the house in the morning for work. She said this had become particularly hard since having children, but it had always been a problem. We agreed that practical support in planning would help with this goal.

Yemi also wanted a goal related to anger. Again, rather than having a goal about the feeling, we focused on the behaviour that resulted from her feeling angry. Yemi said she would like to be able to hold herself back from snapping at her husband when she felt angry.

If clients are finding it hard to decide on or commit to goals, it may help to explain that goal setting is a process of trial and error, and you can 'tweak' them as you go. It is also important to think about their social connections, and things they enjoy and find interesting. We ask about what matters to them – where are or were they happiest? These may be creative projects, sports or going out with friends. Yemi said she would like to make time for herself. Her priority was to go to an exercise class every week; she had not done this since having her children, so one of her goals related to this.

Having identified the goals, we suggest they rate on the scale how much of the time they can do this. Next, we help them break the goals down into subgoals or steps.

Example of breaking down a goal

Yemi wanted to meet the deadlines for her reports at work. We broke it down into steps as follows.

Goal: Complete all reports the day before the deadline.

1.   Find an extra 30 minutes per day for reports.
     •   Put aside the first 45 minutes of the day (when concentration is best and allowing for breaks).
     •   Turn off email and phone.
     •   Do not schedule anything else in this slot wherever possible.

2. Meet with supervisor to discuss the main arguments and agree what to write in each section.
   - Agree regular meeting slots and add to diary.

3. Write one section of the report per day.
   - Set timer to 10-minute intervals (when it went off, she would ask, 'Am I on track?').
   - After 30 minutes (3 × 10 minutes), get a reward (e.g. take a break, have a coffee, chat to a colleague).

This process can be time-consuming so you may choose to do this as you address each goal in turn rather than all at the start. Identifying the sub-goals can be a process of trial and error – if the client is finding it difficult to do these steps, you may need to help them break goals down further.

Session 3 homework: If there is time, ask the client to choose one or two goals to work on before the next session. Then, if you have not done so already, discuss how to break the goal into steps and record these in the relevant section of **Core Handout**: CBT and Adult ADHD. We use the term 'targets' when talking about the weekly tasks and the term 'goals' for the overall therapy goals. Suggest that they complete the first step, or target, before the next session. Agree how the target will be recorded – perhaps using the Therapy Record Form in **Core Handout**: CBT and Adult ADHD or another recording method of the client's choice, for example taking a photo.

Chapter 3 summary
Stage 1: Assessment and Therapy Planning aims to:

- establish a rapport with the client and start to develop the therapeutic alliance
- share the rationale of CBT for ADHD
- co-develop an initial formulation
- instil hope
- agree therapy goals.

In Chapters 4–8 we describe Stage 2: Active Therapy.

CHAPTER 4

Active Therapy

STAGE 2: ACTIVE THERAPY, SESSIONS 4–13

The aims of this stage of therapy are to address the behavioural, emotional and cognitive factors that worsen ADHD challenges and related distress.

It is intended that by the end of therapy, clients have a better understanding of their ADHD and the challenges for which they sought support. This includes knowing what makes challenges better and worse and having strategies to cope with them. Related difficulties such as low confidence and low self-esteem can be directly targeted too. Negative automatic thoughts (NATs), and underlying beliefs about the self, others and the world, will be identified and addressed. In learning the unhelpful effects of old coping behaviours such as avoidance, and unhelpful responses to challenging emotional experiences, clients learn to respond differently. This helps them manage the challenges differently and be less impacted by them and so less distressed.

Given the nature of the condition, ADHD challenges will remain, so it is intended that therapy will foster greater acceptance of challenges and self-compassion for difficult experiences (past and current) as well as an enhanced appreciation of their strengths.

Stage 2: Active Therapy takes place over sessions 4–13 and covers four main topics:

1. Behavioural support to manage challenges including teaching new executive functioning skills, establishing helpful habits and identifying environmental support.
2. NATs – identifying and challenging thoughts.
3. Emotion regulation in relation to unwanted behaviours (e.g. impulsivity and procrastination).
4. Underlying beliefs and coping behaviours.

A typical therapy course would cover the topics in this order. However, the amount of time spent on each – and therefore the session content – will vary between clients, depending on their goals and idiosyncratic formulation. Where challenges and goals primarily relate to managing emotions (e.g. impulsive behaviours or procrastination) or where the client is having difficulty with identifying specific thoughts, we might agree to work on emotions *before* NATs. Sessions will cover more than one topic at a time; for example, behavioural work may continue throughout the sessions even as the thoughts and emotions topics are introduced.

Sessions in Stage 2: Active Therapy follow the same structure as in Stage 1: Assessment and Therapy Planning (see the following box). Sessions last 50 minutes. After a brief update and mood check and bridge from the previous sessions, we agree an agenda. Any homework from the previous session is reviewed, issues on the agenda are discussed and new homework is set, and at the end of the session, we summarize the session and ask for feedback.

Standard CBT session structure
50 minutes

- Brief update and check on mood.
- Bridge from previous session.
- Set agenda.
- Review homework.
- Discuss issues on the agenda.
- Set new homework.
- Summary and feedback.

A mid-therapy review session takes place at approximately session 9 to review progress and to identify and agree on remaining areas to be addressed. It is also an opportunity to discuss any therapy blocks such as non-attendance, late attendance and non-completion of homework.

Here is a summary of the key elements of Stage 2: Active Therapy and the accompanying handouts and homework tasks, along with broad session timings. The four main topic areas of this stage will be described in more detail in the following chapters.

SESSIONS 4–8

BEHAVIOURS

Continue working towards goals – either work on further steps towards the same goals as in the previous sessions or start to work on intermediate targets for some of the other goals on the client's list. Help the client learn practical skills such as time management and organization as required. Use problem-solving strategies with the client for difficulties that arise when working towards goals, for example how to get to work on time. Identify and address ambivalence – discuss the advantages and disadvantages of change.

Handouts:

- **Supplementary Handout**: Activity Diaries
- **Supplementary Handout**: Managing Distractions
- **Supplementary Handout**: Time Management

Homework: Examples include targets for the week guided by the goal list and the intermediate steps, writing and following a daily plan and organization skills. Use the Therapy Record Form to record progress.

NATS

Explain the concept of NATs and how they can worsen ADHD challenges. Help the client to identify idiosyncratic NATs, and to challenge them using Thought Records and behavioural experiments.

Handout:

- **Core Handout**: Thinking Patterns in ADHD

Homework: Continue to work towards targets using the Therapy Record Form to record progress. Record and challenge thoughts using the Thought Record and behavioural experiments.

SESSIONS 9–13

- Mid-therapy review at session 9. Review progress including what has been learned, progress towards goals and any changes in behaviour and thinking. Identify and agree on remaining areas to be addressed. Discuss any therapy blocks.
- Continue working towards goals.

Homework: Use the Therapy Record Form to record progress.

EMOTIONS
Introduce the role of emotions in ADHD. Provide information about emotions, emotion regulation and impulses or action urges. Discuss ways to resist the impulse and the Stop! Stay! Choose! approach.

Handouts:

- **Core Handout**: Managing Emotions and Impulses
- **Supplementary Handout**: Procrastination
- **Supplementary Handout**: Anger

Homework: Complete the Following the impulse and Resisting the impulse diagrams, Impulse Log and Emotion Diary.

UNDERLYING BELIEFS AND COPING BEHAVIOURS
Develop a longitudinal formulation including key core beliefs, rules for living, unhelpful compensatory strategies and their effects. Identify new, more adaptive, core beliefs and rules for living and associated coping strategies. Develop a new formulation with new core beliefs, rules for living and coping strategies. Encourage experimentation with new compensatory strategies. Use behavioural experiments and other cognitive change techniques to find evidence for new beliefs.

Handouts:

- **Core Handout**: Beliefs and Coping
- **Supplementary Handout**: Perfectionism

Homework: Carry out behavioural experiments agreed in the session and compile evidence for new core beliefs.

Chapter 4 summary

The aims of Stage 2: Active Therapy are to address the behavioural, emotional and cognitive factors that worsen ADHD challenges and related distress.

The four main topic areas of Stage 2: Active Therapy will be described in more detail in the following chapters:

- Chapter 5 Behavioural Approaches for ADHD Challenges
- Chapter 6 Thinking Patterns in ADHD
- Chapter 7 Managing Emotions and Impulses
- Chapter 8 Beliefs and Coping

Behavioural Approaches for ADHD Challenges

After discussion of the initial formulation and the goals, early sessions are usually primarily focused on practical behavioural approaches. As clients learn new strategies and habits, they gain confidence, and this builds the therapeutic alliance. Common thinking and behavioural patterns emerge which can be added to the formulation. This deepens the shared understanding of the challenges so we can later address other maintaining factors such as thoughts, beliefs and unhelpful responses to emotional experiences.

Handouts:

- **Supplementary Handout**: Activity Diaries
- **Supplementary Handout**: Managing Distractions
- **Supplementary Handout**: Time Management

At the start of each session, we discuss targets set in the previous session and whether these were met. If the client has met the previous week's targets (if they have managed to do 50–75% of what they planned), they can start the next step or target to work towards the therapy goal. If they have reached the goal, then the homework may be to maintain this. Homework is not given at every session; it depends on what the client and therapist agree is needed to work towards the goals. We can use the Therapy Record Form to record this.

In addressing targets, it may help to discuss daily routines and healthy habits. We can also help the client learn skills such as time management and organization. It may be helpful to introduce environmental adaptations to manage ADHD challenges such as distraction. It may be necessary to engage in problem-solving with the client. We describe these processes in this chapter.

At the end of the chapter, we discuss how to use formulation to further understand the behavioural approaches, including what is working well and any barriers.

DAILY ROUTINES AND HEALTHY HABITS

Even if these are not specified therapy goals, you will want to pay attention to the basics of daily routine and healthy habits. It is assumed that as a CBT therapist, you are well versed in these, so we focus here on the aspects relevant to ADHD. You will be able to draw on knowledge and skills that you have learned as part of behavioural activation for depression.

Many of the challenges of ADHD such as initiating tasks, planning, and inhibiting responses relate to self-regulation. Creating a routine can help with these by reducing 'internal distractions'. For example, consistent sleep and wake times can improve sleep and reduce fatigue. Identifying the best times of day for concentrating can make it easier to stay on task. Routines also help create habits for doing things we enjoy that help us feel good and function at our best. Creating or strengthening habits makes behaviours automatic and reduces the load on executive functioning.

There are several reasons why people with ADHD may not have routines. The executive functioning differences can make it challenging to plan and establish daily habits. Stimulant medication or hyperactivity can lead to a dysregulated sleep cycle. If procrastinating during working hours, people may end up working at other times, leaving less time for leisure activities. People often say they cannot 'legitimately' enjoy downtime, feeling guilty about taking time for themselves when there are things left undone or avoided. They may deliberately delay scheduling enjoyable activities in case they need to make up 'wasted' time. Hyperfocus may lead to getting so wrapped up in something that they lose track of time or forget to eat.

It is helpful to explore thoughts about routine. Many people with ADHD value spontaneity and express concerns that a routine could be overly rigid and strict. They may lack confidence in their ability to stick to a routine having previously tried and not managed. At this stage, it is helpful to use guided discovery to explore the pros and cons of a routine and to think about the different forms a routine can take: does it have to mean a fully structured day or a strict timetable? Is it possible to 'schedule' or allow for unstructured or spontaneous time? Could a routine help them find more time for things they enjoy? If negative automatic thoughts (NATs) are a barrier to the behavioural work, they can be explored further using cognitive techniques such as thought challenging and behavioural experiments (Chapter 6).

We have also noticed some people with ADHD have (usually unrealistically) high expectations for their attention and concentration. This may be because they are sometimes very energetic or able to 'hyperfocus' and so expect this level of performance from themselves *all* the time. We find it helpful to explain that bodies are not machines and brains are not computers. This means they cannot function at the same level all the time. Many things can affect thinking processes including being tired, hungry, upset or stressed and medication wearing off. Once clients understand this, they can make allowances for it. This is not the same as making excuses or letting oneself 'off the hook'; rather, it is about treating oneself with kindness. It allows clients to create the conditions and habits which will help them function at their best.

Activity monitoring

Activity monitoring using activity diaries can show how structured one's time is and how much time is spent, or not, on valued activities. Monitoring can highlight 'boom and bust' behaviour (i.e. intense periods of activity followed by inactivity), irregular sleep and times where they are procrastinating or working extra hours to catch up. It can also illustrate the difference between estimated time for tasks and actual time taken. Activity diaries are difficult for anyone to complete, but the challenges of ADHD can be an extra barrier, so it helps to be flexible in how you use these and only use them where you and the client need to gather specific information about their activity.

If clients cannot complete a whole week, we ask them to complete a day or two. It is important to allow time to discuss how to use the Activity Diary, where they will keep it and what may help them to complete it, i.e. identifying times of day, prompts from others or reminders. We also sometimes complete it retrospectively with them in the session if needed. We usually just ask them to record the main activity for the time slot. The Activity Diary in **Supplementary Handout**: Activity Diaries has two-hour time slots and space to record sleep times. If you need more fine-grained information, you may prefer to use a diary with one-hour slots. If you want to address mood, enjoyment or time spent on valued activities, you may ask them to add ratings of achievement, pleasure or the extent to which they value the activities. Again, if they find it hard to record these things, this difficulty can be explored in conversation in the session instead.

When reviewing the diary, useful questions to ask are: 'What did you notice?', 'Is it what you expected?', 'Is there anything you would like to be doing more or less of?' and 'Do you enjoy...?' Where possible, link it to a therapy goal; for example, 'Your goal is to spend more time with your family – what have you learnt from your Activity Diary about what gets in the way of that?' We sometimes find it helpful to draw pie charts with the client in the session, asking them to show first the proportions of the time they spend on different activities in their day or week now (using different colours for the activities) and then how they would like to spend their time.

Creating routines

Together, identify a routine that balances the priorities and agree weekly targets to try this out. Try changing just one or two things at once. If the client is also low in mood, you can provide information about mood and behavioural activation and work on this at the same time.

Areas to consider

SLEEP

- Consistent getting up and bedtimes.
- Exposure to daylight as early in the day as possible.
- Relaxing evening and bedtime routine, minimizing exposure to blue light from screens.
- Consider the impact of ADHD medication on sleep and, if needed, seek advice from a GP or specialist ADHD clinician on dose timings.
- Avoid or reduce caffeine, nicotine and alcohol for four to six hours before bedtime.

FOOD AND DRINK

- Healthy diet and regular mealtimes. There are no specific nutrition guidelines for ADHD. The advice is the same as for the general population, i.e. to eat a balanced, varied diet and to eat at regular intervals. ADHD challenges can affect what clients eat, what they buy and when they buy it – they may miss meals, find it hard to cook meals and spend excess money on takeaways or deliveries.

EXERCISE AND MOVEMENT

- High energy levels and feelings of internal restlessness or agitation are helped by regular exercise and movement. This may include formal exercise sessions such as running, sports or yoga but also other motor activity such as fidget toys, chewing gum, moving around or dancing. Again, what is felt to be helpful is highly individual. The important things are both to explore with the client what they already find helpful, helping them implement this in a consistent way, and to encourage them to experiment with new strategies as needed.

WORK, CHORES, OBLIGATIONS

- Ring-fence time for important tasks so they do not take over.
- Schedule breaks.
- Identify typical attention span and times of day when concentration is best. You can use information from the Activity Diary to help with this. If they do not know, you can encourage them to experiment with concentrating for different time spans using a timer. It helps to start with relatively short time spans (sometimes even a minute at first) and from there gradually increase the concentration target time.

LEISURE ACTIVITIES

- Social connections, relaxation, cultural and creative activities and hobbies.

As you explore these elements, you and the client may discover more about what gets in the way of their valued activities. For example, there may be challenges in their social relationships such as fears of negative evaluation or rejection. These might be areas that the client would like further support with and for which the cognitive and emotional approaches would be helpful (see Chapters 6, 7 and 8).

Forming new habits

When setting the weekly targets, you are often helping the client to form new habits. It can help to link the new target to existing habits, such as breakfast or brushing teeth, by doing them directly before or after. It may also help to be prompted by, or to do them alongside, a family member. Alarms and phone reminders can prompt new habits.

It takes time and regular practice to form new habits. You can use the Therapy Record Form to record progress. Even once targets are being met most of the time, it is a good idea for the client to continue to record them for a few weeks to help embed new habits. These can be reviewed in session and further support can be given as needed.

Reward versus self-criticism

The process of setting therapy goals and breaking them down into smaller weekly targets shows the client how to set small, achievable targets. It is helpful to hold in mind the behavioural principles of conditioning that underlie CBT so that we can teach clients how to use reward to motivate themselves and establish their new habits (see Table 2).

Table 2: Operant conditioning contingencies

Operant conditioning		
	Add something (+)	Remove something (–)
Increase a behaviour (+)	Positive reinforcement (reward)	Negative reinforcement
Decrease a behaviour (–)	Positive punishment	Negative punishment

Behaviours become linked to their consequences. A pleasant consequence or reward (positive reinforcement) makes a behaviour more likely to be repeated. Clients may think rewards are unnecessary or even undeserved, so it is helpful to provide this information and challenge this belief. We encourage clients to focus on what has gone well, rewarding all new habits and steps towards their goals. We also explain that smaller, frequent rewards are likely to be more effective than bigger, longer-term ones, and we help them write a list of rewards. The Rewards and Enjoyable Activities worksheet in **Core Handout**: CBT and Adult

ADHD guides the client in writing a list of rewards and enjoyable activities. This includes daily activities that they could do throughout the day, weekly activities, occasional activities and activities that they can do to motivate them to start activities or stay on track. If the client needs ideas, there are numerous lists of pleasant activities online.

Many people believe that criticizing themselves (positive punishment) helps them get things done and avoid complacency. In fact, self-criticism is not only less powerful than reward, but it also makes the task aversive, increasing anxiety, avoidance and disorganization. This is because it does not teach what *to do*, only what *not to do*. So, using Socratic dialogue, we explore the effect on them of focusing on what they have *not* done or on wider struggles and explore the advantages instead of giving oneself credit for progress in the right direction, however small it may seem. We also help them notice and challenge self-critical thoughts (Chapter 6).

STRATEGIES TO HELP WITH ATTENTION

Here are some ways to adapt the surroundings and some external tools to help with attention and memory.

Reduce distractions
Workspace

- Keep a tidy workspace.
- Face the desk away from distractions, e.g. a window or busy room.

Electronic devices

- Turn the phone over, use airplane mode or keep it in a different room.
- Limit the number of open tabs, reduce notifications and use 'do not disturb' settings.

Sounds:

- Reduce background noise or use headphones or earplugs.
- Alternatively, add sound – this is highly personal so encourage experimentation with:
  - music or spoken word radio/podcasts

- white, brown or pink noise – these are sounds of different frequency ranges, available to stream online.

Accommodations for additional sensory sensitivities

- Light (bright lights or certain wavelengths).
- Temperature.
- Touch (e.g. wearing soft, comfortable clothing).

Use 'external' tools to support executive functions

If we try and keep too many things in mind at once, then we use valuable working memory to think of them when we are trying to concentrate on other things. For this reason, it helps to support thinking where possible using the following strategies:

Write things down

Use tools such as diaries, 'to-do' lists (see the 'Time management' section later in this chapter), shopping lists and notes.

Cues, prompts and reminders

These can take numerous forms. It may help to display signs and notes around the house, such as a note on the front door reminding them to take their keys. A family member or partner may be able to remind them to do something, such as to take medication or take a break to go for a walk. Electronic reminders and alarms on the phone, computer or smart speaker can prompt them to do something, interrupt a period of 'hyperfocus' where they may be stuck on one task or remind them to get back on task when distracted. There are also apps available to help people establish and maintain habits.

A timer

This has a few functions. First, it can be used as a prompt to regulate attention. It can be set for short intervals to bring back attention when it wanders. We suggest clients try to accept mind-wandering as normal and 'OK' rather than criticizing themselves and use the timer as a prompt to move back on task. Starting with small chunks – a minute at a time if necessary – they can gradually increase the time as their concentration span improves.

They can also use a timer to set a specific amount of time to complete a task. They may be surprised by how productive they can be in just a few minutes of focused work. This can be used in behavioural experiments to challenge perfectionism or beliefs that they need to allow a certain amount of time to start a task (such 'permission giving' beliefs are common in procrastination, e.g. 'I need a free afternoon before I can start that'). When the timer goes off, they can choose a reward from their reward list.

Clients who underestimate how long things take may find it helpful to note the estimated and actual task timings to learn to allocate realistic time frames.

Supplementary Handout: Managing Distractions summarizes these ideas and invites the client to note what they have tried already and what has worked or not worked. They may find it helpful to discuss this further. For example, clients typically say that things that get in the way of making notes include:

- wanting the 'perfect' notes system (and abandoning it when it is not quite right)
- losing devices or notebooks
- starting multiple lists or systems and then losing track.

If some approaches have not worked, explore this with them and problem-solve if possible. It can help them to identify and, if necessary, challenge their thoughts about these. Next, help them identify ways to use them more consistently; for example, deciding on a place to keep the notebook and a time to look at it every day.

Seek support

- If the client has a manager, they may be able to provide further support, either with the job itself in the form of help with structuring time and workload or with putting in place reasonable adjustments, or both (see Chapter 10 for more information about workplace support).

- If the client is self-employed, it may be possible to access guidance via peer support or mentorship.

- Adults with ADHD in the UK who are in work, self-employed or about to start work may be entitled to fully funded support (such as coaching) from the government disability scheme known as Access to Work (see Chapter 10).

- Working alongside another person either in person or virtually, known as 'body doubling', can help people stay on task. ADHD support groups offer body doubling spaces on video calls, and there are also live streams online of people working.

TIME MANAGEMENT

When we talk about time management, we mean an approach for completing non-routine specific tasks rather than the routine activities of daily living, though they overlap. Not all clients will want or need to discuss time management. Time management support may be indicated if the client reports missing appointments or deadlines or feeling overwhelmed by things to do and not knowing how to approach them.

Supplementary Handout: Time Management describes a step-by-step process based on the ABC method of assigning priorities to tasks (Lakein, 1973). Some people do not know the principles of time management and find the information helpful. Even then, this approach is just a suggestion, and the client may not want to follow it completely. Many of our clients have used it as a starting point for their own experiments to find out what works for them.

The following case example uses the time management approach for a fictional self-employed client called Mel.

Case example: Mel

Mel is a furniture maker and has her own business. She hopes to make a living from the business but it is not making money.

Two of her therapy goals related to time management:

- Make a plan for every day.
- Follow the plan.

We identified the following smaller steps:

- Check diary for appointments the night before.

- Make a plan the night before.
- Since she wanted to work four hours per day, she included this in the plan and also included adequate breaks and rewards.
- Mel worked better when she had company (body doubling) so she would message her work friend Tim the night before to make sure he was at the workshop the next day.

We marked these as individual targets on the weekly target achievement chart.

We then devised a plan together for the following day, assigning priorities and timings:

Mel's plan:

What to do	Priority	Estimated time
Tidy workshop	A	3 hours
Meet Tim to discuss job	A	30 minutes
Hang pictures	C	1 hour
Tidy desk at home	B	30 minutes
In addition – travel to and from workshop: 20 minutes		

Breaks and rewards:

- Coffee/tea/snack
- Lunch
- TV

We then assigned an order:

9.30am: Travel to workshop
10–12pm: Tidy workshop – break for coffee at 11am for 10 minutes
12–1pm: Meet Tim over lunch
1–2pm: Tidy workshop
2–2.30pm: Travel home
2.30–3.30pm: Break – watch TV with a snack and cup of tea
3.30–4pm: Tidy desk
4–5pm: Hang pictures

Mel then noted what happened – whether she followed or missed out parts of the plan. We agreed she could try to observe non-judgementally and notice whether she criticized herself.

In the next session, she explained that she'd got everything done but not at the exact times in the plan. Tim was at the workshop, but he was busy and could not meet her for lunch, so they agreed to meet the next day, and she went for a walk instead. She needed Tim's help to lift some furniture, so that also had to wait until the next day. She reflected that she needed deadlines up to a point, but deadlines needed to be flexible to accommodate other people and changes in the plan. Overall, she was pleased with how things had gone and said that as she'd got things done, she'd noticed the thought 'I can get things done' and her mood was more hopeful.

Sometimes clients express doubts about time management, saying they do not want to feel restricted or they value spontaneity. If this is the case, we gently explore the pros and cons with them and invite them to experiment. Does it have to be 'all or nothing'? Could they, perhaps, structure just some of the day/week, leaving time for more unstructured or spontaneous activity?

Very often people know the principles of time management but struggle to put them into practice. **Supplementary Handout**: Time Management may inform discussions about what they have tried so far, what has worked, or not, and what gets in the way. This will be different for each person, and the formulation will help you develop an individual approach.

For example, Mel realized that one of the things that prevented her from making a daily plan was that she found it hard to make decisions. When we explored this, she said she wanted to keep her 'options open' (which we later linked to perfectionism). As we discussed the advantages and disadvantages of planning ahead, she realized there would be more to gain than to lose from doing this: 'The advantages of waiting to decide are that I will have more information and I will make better decisions. Because of the way I think – slowly – I need to take time to decide. This way, I don't create a mess for the future, and I can create something that I am proud of. But the disadvantages are that it takes a long time, it feels daunting, I plan less and I can't get as much done.'

She concluded that it would be helpful to experiment with adding one small thing from her to-do list to her daily plan every day 'without overthinking it' and to 'settle with good enough'. After trying this, she reported that she had managed to do one thing from her to-do list every day, felt good about this and started to feel more comfortable with planning ahead.

ORGANIZATION

There are numerous strategies for organization available online and in other therapy manuals (see Chapter 12 for further resources). They mainly relate to organizing belongings and paperwork or digital files. Your client may already know of some of these, and you can look them up as needed.

The aim is not to repeat that information here but to think about how to use a formulation-driven approach to help clients engage with organizational strategies and how to identify what gets in the way. Understanding this will help clients establish and maintain new helpful organizational behaviours so they can self-manage in the future.

The key principles of organizing include finding places to keep key items, grouping similar items together and forming habits around putting things in their place. Organizational systems and habits are most likely to work if they are simple and easy to use, accessible (i.e. easy to get to/reach) and visible and do not take too long. They also need to be used consistently. Executive functioning differences make implementation difficult so think about tools such as visual prompts, timers, notes, diary reminders and support from a partner or family member.

The client may feel overwhelmed and not know where to start in addressing organization. Remember you do not need to do it all. To keep goals around organization manageable, identify one or two things that would be different if they were organized.

> For example, Ali wanted to take everything that he needed to college. To put this into practice, we identified all the things that needed to happen to result in him taking what he needed. Another way to do this is to think about the ways in which it goes *awry*, i.e. what does *not* happen. The things that needed to happen and ways he could do these were as follows:
>
> **Remember what to take to college** → write list.

Know where these are → decide on set places for the bag and its contents.

Remember to pack the bag, including checking the diary → set reminder on the phone in the session.

Know where the packed bag is → leave by the front door.

This discussion resulted in the goal and subgoals below.

Goal: Take everything I need to college

1. Write a list of everything needed: wallet, keys, ID badge, phone, water bottle, etc.
2. Decide where to keep the bag and its contents (by the front door) and where to keep the wallet and keys (on a small shelf in the hallway).
3. Write anything extra needed for college in the diary.
4. Set a phone reminder to pack the bag the night before, including checking the diary for extra items.
5. Leave the bag by the front door, the wallet and keys on the shelf and pick them up before leaving.

REVIEWING TARGETS

Having agreed behavioural targets for the client to complete between sessions, the next step is to review them. Ask about them in the following session. Ask about what worked, being sure to ask about the successes. The client may discount these or criticize themselves, and in this case, gently help them notice this, if possible, encouraging a more positive or balanced interpretation of events.

What has been learnt?

A key aim of this stage is for the client to learn new skills and habits. We want to encourage a spirit of exploration and experimentation. It helps to ask what did not work, reminding them that you had both anticipated this and can learn just as much from what *did not* happen as what *did* happen. As you work out together what got in the way, you can think of ways to refine the target for next time. There may be practical solutions – for example if they forgot to do it, they need help with prompts and reminders.

In addition to new skills and habits, behavioural interventions can, of course, also lead to cognitive change. When discussing homework, it helps to make explicit any cognitive change by asking, 'What did you learn?' Homework tasks can be used as formal behavioural experiments with a worksheet. You can, of course, use a similar process but informally in conversation – for example, 'What did you predict was going to happen? Is that what happened? What do you think now about your statement, "I can't..."?' Where possible, elicit new thoughts/beliefs about self-efficacy and control. We saw this in the example of Mel experimenting with using time management which led to her changing her beliefs from 'I need to take time to decide on the *right* plan' to 'I get more done if I choose one thing every day and do it to a *good enough* standard.'

Going 'off track' and getting back on track

One of the key parts of learning self-management is noticing and responding when things do not go to plan. This is a good opportunity to highlight any perfectionism and introduce the idea of flexibility. It is not possible to complete targets 100% of the time; similarly, getting distracted or getting carried away (hyperfocus) is to be expected. The most important thing is to notice what has happened and bring themselves back on track with compassion. With practice, they will notice more quickly and get back on track more quickly. Discuss with them how they can notice going off track; help them talk to themselves kindly when it happens. Problem-solve it – could prompts, reminders or timers keep them on track? Would it help to experiment with staying on track for shorter time frames?

Using formulation to help with behaviour change

At this stage, it can be helpful to draw out a five areas model with the client, noticing the thoughts, behaviours, emotions and physical sensations that arose, perhaps when they thought about doing something they needed to do or when they realized they had not done something they intended to do. You may identify NATs and beliefs that can be addressed, for example self-criticism, perfectionism, fears of failure or negative thoughts about uncertainty. There may be uncomfortable emotions such as anxiety, boredom or shame. You can then help the client understand how these are related to behaviours such as avoidance that prevent them from doing the things they want to do.

For example, Ali had managed to implement our agreed plan to take everything to college on one out of two days over the previous week. We explored this further. He explained that on the day that it did not happen, he had had a busy day at work and was feeling tired when he came home. A friend messaged to ask whether he wanted to game. He said packing his bag went through his mind, but he thought, 'I don't need to do it yet', 'That's boring' and, 'I deserve a bit of a break, then I'll do it.' When asked about the effect of those thoughts, he said they led to 'ignoring' the bag (avoidance); instead, he ended up gaming all evening and then had some food and went to bed late and without packing. We explored some practical steps to help him with packing the bag. These included asking his mum to gently remind him to do it as soon as he got home before relaxing for the evening.

Such conversations will guide your therapy plan. You may decide to cover thought challenging (Chapter 6) next (Ali's next step was to learn to notice and challenge the thoughts that interrupted his plans) or, if managing uncomfortable emotional experiences is the main challenge, for instance in the case of procrastination or impulsive behaviours, you may decide to move on to the emotions topic first (Chapter 7).

Chapter 5 summary

This chapter covered behavioural approaches which are the focus of the early sessions in Stage 2: Active Therapy.

- Targets are set and reviewed each session. They may include:
  - daily routines and healthy habits
  - skills such as time management and organization
  - environmental adaptations to manage ADHD challenges.
- Information about reward and enjoyable activities is provided.
- Formulation allows us to identify and address thoughts and emotions that prevent the client from implementing targets.

CHAPTER 6

Thinking Patterns in ADHD

Handout:

- **Core Handout**: Thinking Patterns in ADHD

There is emerging evidence that ADHD is associated with negative automatic thoughts (NATs). One study found that adults with ADHD have significantly more NATs than those in a non-clinical control sample even when controlling for co-morbid depression (Mitchell *et al.*, 2013). Adults with ADHD score highly on measures of negative thinking including perfectionism (Strohmeier *et al.*, 2016). Adults with ADHD also report higher perceived criticism from others compared with those without the condition and less self-compassion (Beaton, Sirois and Milne, 2020). Further research is needed, but these studies suggest that directly targeting NATs could be an important component of CBT for adult ADHD.

COMMON NATS IN ADHD

We have observed that NATs in ADHD commonly fall into two main areas:

1. Lack of confidence in ability to achieve tasks or goals, self-control and reliability.

Growing up with ADHD, people may have received negative feedback. Even if they have not received overt feedback, they may have felt different to, or negatively compared themselves with, classmates or siblings without the same challenges. These experiences can result in unhelpful or biased thoughts about their abilities.

For example:

'I am out of control.'
'I have let others down.'
'I will never be able to do this.'

2. High personal standards and self-criticism.

People with ADHD may be prone to making high demands of themselves. They may criticize themselves for mistakes or things that they have not done. They may set unrealistic goals, leading to further self-criticism when those goals are not met
For example:

'I always mess things up.'
'What a stupid thing to do.'
'I should have done that better.'
'It is ridiculous that I can't do this.'

ADDRESSING NATS

You will have already introduced the role of cognitions in ADHD when sharing the rationale for CBT and co-developing the initial formulation in Stage 1: Assessment and Therapy Planning, and you may have highlighted some NATs. You may have also noticed and 'informally' challenged NATs when working towards behavioural targets by experimenting with new habits and testing out thoughts such as 'This won't work for me.' If we use structured cognitive techniques such as Thought Records or behavioural experiments to explore NATs, we usually do this once the client has been working towards behavioural targets for at least a session or two.

Core Handout: Thinking Patterns in ADHD explains the role of NATs and introduces the five areas model, categories of thinking biases and thought challenging. Depending on the client's preferences and needs, you can give this as reading before the session or you may read it with the client in the session. Either way, we would usually complete the five areas diagram together in the session.

We start by asking the client about a recent example of one of their ADHD challenges or when they noticed a shift in mood. Using the blank diagram in Image A5 (**Core Handout:** Thinking Patterns in ADHD), we note together the thoughts, emotions, physical reactions and behaviours and the links between them. As with CBT for any condition, it is important to distinguish between NATs, which are situation specific, and core beliefs, which are more general and usually require different techniques to modify them.

USING A THOUGHT RECORD

If the client can access their thoughts, then it may be helpful to provide information about thinking biases and explore thoughts further using a Thought Record. Depending on how easy they find this, further Thought Records can be completed independently for homework or with guidance from you in the session.

Many people have had difficult experiences because of ADHD, and many have been criticized, so questioning the evidence for and against the NAT may not be helpful. Instead, it may be more beneficial to explore the effects of the thinking and the advantages and disadvantages. This also helps if thinking is stuck or rigid. We adapted the Thought Record form in Appendix 2 to make clearer the links between thinking and the resulting physical sensations, emotions and behaviours. It includes the unhelpful behaviours and their consequences, and in the 're-frame' section, more helpful behaviours.

We found that the following questions are helpful to ask when re-framing the hot thought (the thought that causes the most emotional distress):

1. Is this a thought or a fact?
   a. What evidence is there for the thought?
   b. Is there any evidence against the thought?
   c. Can you spot any thinking biases?
2. What would you say to a friend of yours if they thought the same?
3. Is it possible you are only seeing one part of the situation and ignoring other factors (such as your strengths or positives in the situation)?
4. Are you blaming yourself for something that you cannot control?
5. What are the advantages of thinking this way?
   ...and what are the disadvantages of thinking this way?
6. What do you feel in your body and what do you want to do when you have this thought?
7. Does this thought move you towards or away from your goal

(of...)? Is there another way of thinking about this that would move you towards your goal (i.e. make your desired behaviour more likely to happen)?

See the example of the completed Thought Record for Yemi who was finding it difficult to get ready in the morning.

DECIDING WHETHER TO USE THOUGHT RECORDS

As in any condition, in ADHD Thought Records are not always the most appropriate intervention. The client's formulation will indicate whether NATs are the drivers of the client's distress. If unwanted behaviours or strong emotions are the main challenges, you may decide to focus instead on the behavioural approaches (Chapter 5), managing emotions (Chapter 7) and beliefs and coping (Chapter 8) topics of Stage 2: Active Therapy, which focus more on behaviour change. Thought Records may nonetheless be a useful tool to gather more data for your formulation. You may also find it helpful to return to them later in therapy – for example, you can use them after formulating procrastination (Chapter 7) to then address self-critical or perfectionist thinking.

Even if Thought Records are appropriate for your client, simply challenging is usually not enough. The best way to test out the validity of the new thought is to try it in day-to-day life (Padesky and Greenberger, 1995). There is evidence to suggest that behavioural experiments may be more powerful for some people than Thought Records (McManus, Van Doorn and Yiend, 2012). You can use behavioural experiment record forms if you wish, or simply discuss thoughts and beliefs when planning and reviewing behavioural homework tasks. As you and the client identify thoughts and beliefs that maintain ADHD challenges and unhelpful coping, you can help them test the validity or 'helpfulness' of the thoughts and beliefs, noting how these change after they do something differently.

This will usually be doing something that that the client thinks they cannot do, does not want to do or predicts will be too boring, etc. For example, after finding a way to pack his bag as soon as he got home from work, Ali realized his thoughts had changed from 'I don't need to do this yet' and 'It is too boring' to 'If I don't do this now, I'll forget.' Overall, he learnt: 'Even though it's boring, I can do it – it will only take me five minutes and then I can relax.'

Yemi's completed Thought Record

Situation	Thought	Emotion	Physical	Behaviour	Consequence?
	What went through your mind? Rate belief in 'hot' thought (0–100%) Can you spot any thinking biases?	What emotions were around? Rate emotion (0–100%)	What did you feel in your body? Rate intensity (0–100%)	What did you do/ what do you want to do?	What happened?
Took three times longer than my husband to get ready this morning	I haven't got anything done (all or nothing, discounting the positives) I am going to let him down 80% (catastrophizing, fortune-telling)	Irritable 70% Flat 60% Sad 60%	Heavy 70%	Withdraw Hide my feelings Tell myself off	I spent the morning dwelling on it Felt worse, more distractible than usual

→

Re-frame

	Thought	Emotion	Physical	Behaviour	
	Alternative thought	What emotions are around now? Re-rate emotion (0–100%)	What can you feel in your body now? Rate intensity (0–100%)	What can you do now?	
	I have got some things done We are different, we contribute in different ways Telling myself off just makes me feel worse and makes it harder – I am trying the best I can Belief in hot thought 50%	Irritable 40% Flat 25% Sad 40%	A bit lighter Heavy 45%	Plan for tomorrow morning this evening so I know what I need to do	

Chapter 6 summary

- There is evidence that ADHD is associated with NATs.
- The five areas model and Thought Records help clients identify and address NATs.
- We test the validity of thoughts by asking clients to note how thoughts change following behaviour change.

CHAPTER 7

Managing Emotions and Impulses

Handouts:

- **Core Handout**: Managing Emotions and Impulses
- **Supplementary Handout**: Procrastination
- **Supplementary Handout**: Anger

In this chapter we discuss common ADHD challenges of impulsive or unwanted behaviours, such as procrastination, in relation to emotion regulation. Impulsivity and procrastination may seem like opposite problems but there is evidence that they are moderately positively correlated and relate to self-regulation (Steel, 2007).

We usually move on to this stage after addressing behaviour (Chapter 5) and negative automatic thoughts (NATs) (Chapter 6). However, if the client's challenges and goals relate primarily to managing emotional experiences, you may decide to start here or move on to this section after the behavioural approaches. An indication for this would be if the client is asking for support with unwanted behaviours that cause distress to themselves and others and feel 'out of control'. This can include a wide range of behaviours that include spending money without thinking, avoiding or putting off tasks, gaming, gambling, spending time on the internet (including social media), sex, overeating or having emotional outbursts.

Core Handout: Managing Emotions and Impulses may be useful even if the client is not describing impulsivity as such. For example, in procrastination, challenging emotional experiences may be characterized by demotivation or fatigue rather than a drive *towards* action. We suggest you read the handout before starting to discuss this topic with your clients. It includes the following information.

- Many people with ADHD report challenges in managing their emotional experiences.
- Impulsive or unwanted behaviours often result from unhelpful ways of managing emotional experiences.
- In understanding more about their emotional experiences, they can learn to resist the impulses or action urges that lead to unwanted behaviours and respond in alternative, more helpful ways.

The earlier sections of the handout provide information about emotions, including the function of emotions and common beliefs about emotions that can lead to unhelpful ways of coping with them. This is because this information is an important basis for the later sections that focus on responding to emotional experiences in new ways.

When introducing the topic, however, we often start by talking with the client about the behaviours themselves and introduce the idea that these unwanted behaviours may follow from *unhelpful ways of responding to emotional experiences.* First, we ask them about a recent experience where their actions felt out of control, perhaps because they behaved in a way that they did not like or which had negative results for them. Examples might be spending too much money impulsively or having an emotional outburst. If their goal is to address procrastination, we ask them about that. Procrastination is not necessarily related to feeling out of control, but it is, like impulsive behaviours, often related to difficult emotional experiences.

First, we complete the blank Following the impulse diagram (Image A10 from **Core Handout**: Managing Emotions and Impulses) with them using one of their recent examples. (Note that there is a **Supplementary Handout**: Procrastination, but it is helpful for the client to read **Core Handout**: Managing Emotions and Impulses first, as the ideas in the **supplementary handout** follow on from those in the core handout.)

Responses become maintained if, in the short term, they are positively or negatively *reinforced*. This is where something that feels good happens – for example the rush of pleasure when buying something – or something that feels bad goes away or reduces – for example the feelings of uncertainty or discomfort around a task when procrastinating.

As we complete the Following the Impulse diagram, the client sees how the short-term consequences of the behaviour are reinforcing. They see that it is understandable that they have come to cope with challenging emotional experiences in this way, since they immediately feel better when they do. This conceptualization can counteract confusion and shame.

We then explore with the client how a response that feels good or relieves discomfort in the short term may lead to distress in the longer term. They identify the thoughts and feelings that result from their action or inaction – there may be guilt, shame or regret. They identify that the situation will not be resolved, or may even be worse, and that they feel less confident in their ability to cope.

Core Handout: Managing Emotions and Impulses and Image 2 illustrate this process using Ali's example of impulsive spending, showing the role of the short-term and longer-term consequences in maintaining the cycle.

Following the impulse

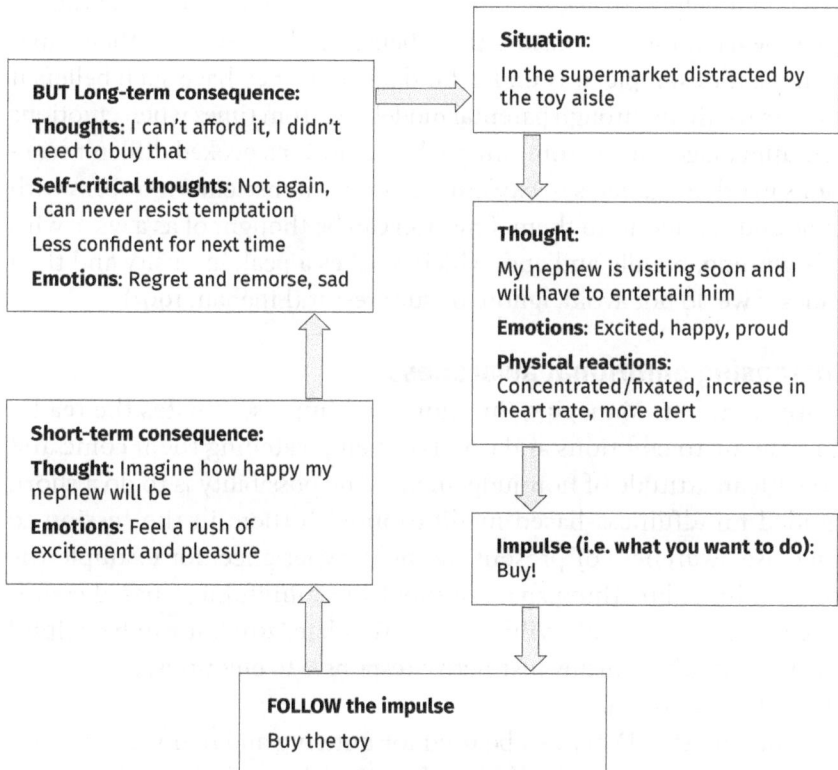

Situation:
In the supermarket distracted by the toy aisle

BUT Long-term consequence:
Thoughts: I can't afford it, I didn't need to buy that
Self-critical thoughts: Not again, I can never resist temptation
Less confident for next time
Emotions: Regret and remorse, sad

Thought:
My nephew is visiting soon and I will have to entertain him
Emotions: Excited, happy, proud
Physical reactions:
Concentrated/fixated, increase in heart rate, more alert

Short-term consequence:
Thought: Imagine how happy my nephew will be
Emotions: Feel a rush of excitement and pleasure

Impulse (i.e. what you want to do):
Buy!

FOLLOW the impulse
Buy the toy

Image 2: Ali's impulsive spending example using the Following the impulse diagram

We usually give the client the handout to read for homework and discuss with them in the following sessions the information it contains about emotions and ways of managing them. We will now describe the rest of **Core Handout**: Managing Emotions and Impulses in the order the information is presented.

FACTS ABOUT EMOTIONS

Since unwanted behaviours can result from unhelpful ways of managing challenging emotional experiences, learning *helpful* responses to emotional experiences may help in managing those unwanted behaviours.

Beliefs about emotions

Some people have unhelpful beliefs about emotions such as that they will go on for a long time or that they are unacceptable or unbearable. We find it helpful to ask the client whether they have any beliefs about their own emotions. Consider these beliefs in the context of their experiences; for example, it is understandable that they have such beliefs if they learnt them through parental modelling, from times when emotions felt unmanageable or from times when emotions evoked difficult reactions in others. It helps to explain that even intense emotions pass with time and cannot harm them. Emotion can be thought of as a wave with a beginning, middle and end, which reaches a peak intensity and then fades if we do not avoid, ignore or suppress it (Linehan, 1993).

Increasing emotional awareness

Core Handout: Managing Emotions and Impulses invites the reader to 'tune in' to emotions and observe them, watching them come and go with an attitude of non-judgement. One possibility is to do a short, guided mindfulness-based meditation with them in the session to increase awareness of present moment experience, for example the three-minute breathing space, a tool from mindfulness-based cognitive therapy (see Segal, Williams and Teasdale, 2012). It can be helpful to explore with them any instinctive responses to emotions, even if they did not act on them.

The Emotion Diary can be used for noticing and naming emotions as they arise. As with the rest of the general population, adults with ADHD vary in the degree to which they can identify or name emotions and so some may need extra help. If so, you can give further education about emotions and labelling emotions. Some people find it easier to notice the accompanying physical sensations. They may find it helpful to use 'body-mapping', that is, a line drawing of a human body where they can place colours, words or symbols to represent how emotions feel in the body. Emotion wheels can support learning about emotions and are available online, though they vary. Plutchik's Wheel of Emotions illustrates primary emotions, secondary emotions and their relationships to behavioural patterns (Plutchik, 2001); however, a drawback in relation to ADHD is that it does not include shame. The Feeling Wheel (Willcox, 1982) includes only emotions but can be helpful in identifying and accepting emotional experiences.

Emotion regulation

Core Handout: Managing Emotions and Impulses includes information about emotion regulation. It explains that some strategies may be practised even when calm, others in anticipation of difficult situations and still others to help manage emotional experiences once they have been triggered.

It is helpful to share with clients strategies for managing emotional and physiological arousal levels. This overlaps with some of the healthy habits covered in Chapter 5. We have found it helpful to offer psychoeducation about *hyper* (over) and *hypo* (under) arousal and to support clients to recognize and respond to these states in specific situations.

We often share the Window of Tolerance metaphor (Siegel, 1999; Siegel 2024) to help understand emotional experiences and explore ways of managing them. The 'window' refers to an optimal zone of emotional and physical arousal where we feel calm, process information and manage emotions and behaviour to the best of our ability. People have different sized windows depending on experience, life stressors and other factors such as neurodivergence, which can increase emotional sensitivity. The size of the window is situation-specific and idiosyncratic – for example someone's window may be narrower for anger than for sadness. Outside of this zone there is a limited ability to respond to or tolerate emotional experiences. This can result in either chaos – being flooded, excessively stressed, overwhelmed disorganized and 'at our limits' – or rigidity – withdrawal, shutting down, becoming closed off, numbing out, disconnecting and having 'tunnel vision'. Hyper arousal is often associated with chaos and hypo arousal is often associated with rigidity, however they do not correspond exactly, for example the freeze state is a result of hyper arousal while the faint state is a result of hypo arousal (see Siegel 2024 for more information).

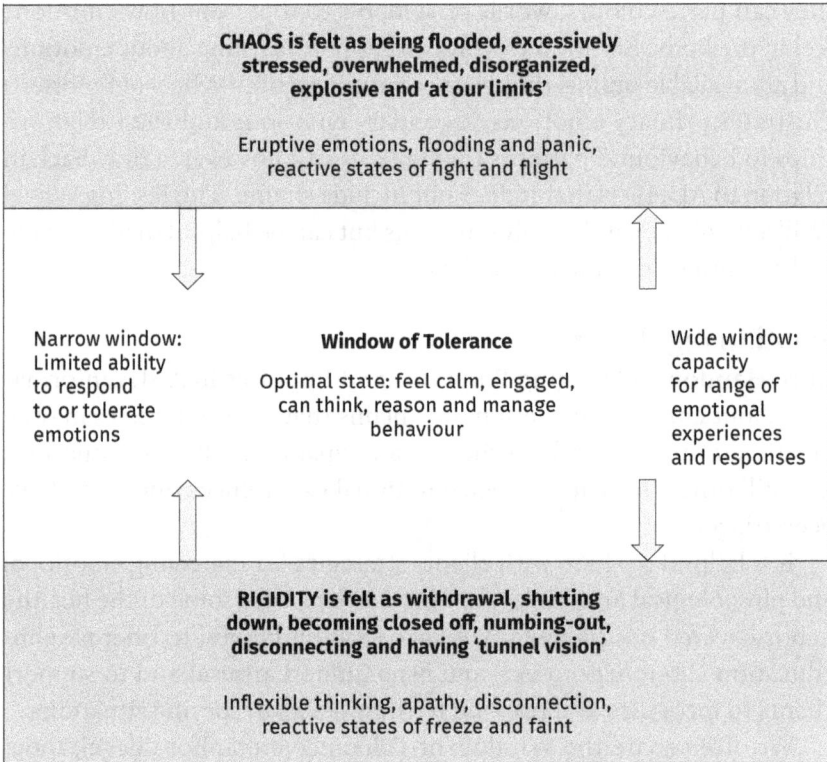

Image A6: Window of Tolerance (Adapted from Siegel 2024)

We can expand the window and therefore become more able to experience and respond helpfully to emotions, feeling more resilient and resourceful under stress. This involves recognizing arousal states and finding ways to manage them. Note: hyper and hypo are not the same as being outside the window. High levels of intensity can be *helpful* for some people, helping them to feel comfortable and think clearly and indeed many people with ADHD report this. It is also possible to be in a state of hypo arousal or deep relaxation and be able to function well. Nonetheless if someone needs to reduce the intensity of their physical or emotional state to get back into the window, helpful responses are soothing, calming and grounding. These can be learned via exercises that help clients to engage with the present moment such as deep breathing, mindfulness-based exercises, grounding techniques to reduce arousal levels such as relaxation (progressive muscle relaxation or guided imagery) or sensory self-soothing activities. Conversely, if they need to increase arousal levels to return to the window, it may help to engage in stimulating activities such as sensory stimulation (e.g. smelling essential oils, eating crunchy food), moving one's body or listening to uplifting or energizing music.

Formulation, education, identifying and challenging beliefs about emotions and simple emotional regulation skills tend to be sufficient to support clients with ADHD in exposure to avoided emotional states and embedding new responses. Of course, if the client has a trauma history, it may be very distressing for them to feel emotions that they have avoided or suppressed, and more extensive support with emotion regulation may be needed.

RESPONDING TO IMPULSES AND ACTION URGES

Emotions have associated action urges. For simplicity, in **Core Handout**: Managing Emotions and Impulses, we refer to these as 'impulses' (and later to 'following and resisting the impulse'). In some circumstances these action urges or impulses are helpful – for example, avoiding or running away from danger can keep us safe. This is sometimes known as the 'fight or flight' response. We have these instinctive responses because they helped our ancestors survive, and our ancestors passed on their genes to us. A response that may be protective in some situations may cause problems in others – for example, avoiding situations that provoke anxiety may lead to procrastination. It is therefore the context that determines whether a response is helpful or unhelpful.

WHAT MAKES IMPULSE PROBLEMS WORSE?

Core Handout: Managing Emotions and Impulses explains how unhelpful responses become maintained. It shows the role of the short-term and longer-term consequences in maintaining the cycle as has already been explored with the client in the previous session when discussing their own example, and it provides some further examples.

RESISTING IMPULSES USING THE STOP! STAY! CHOOSE! STRATEGY

Core Handout: Managing Emotions and Impulses then introduces the Stop! Stay! Choose! strategy to resist the impulse. We encourage clients to notice when they are about to follow, are following or have just followed an impulse. Drawing on recently introduced emotion regulation skills, we invite them to stop and stay with the impulse, that is, to experience all elements of the emotional experience (thoughts, emotions, physical reactions). This facilitates exposure to the specific emotional state. Finally, we help them interrupt or resist the impulse and identify and experiment with alternative responses. **Core Handout:** Managing Emotions and Impulses illustrates this using the example of Ali's impulsive spending.

You can use the blank Resisting the impulse diagram to map out what happens when the client resists rather than follows the impulse. Resisting the impulse leads to different short-term and long-term consequences from following the impulse. This in turn can then lead to new emotional experiences (thoughts, emotions, physical reactions) when they encounter similar situations in the future.

An Impulse Log is included in **Core Handout:** Managing Emotions and Impulses to note what happens when practising the Stop! Stay! Choose! strategy over the following weeks. The client is invited to note all the parts of the emotional experience (thoughts, emotions, physical reactions) when resisting impulses. If the client can identify emotions, see if they can rate them at the time of the impulse, immediately on using the Stop! Stay! Choose! approach and then a bit later (short- and long-term consequences of resisting the impulse). There are prompts on the log for the client to think about different salient aspects of the experience (thoughts, physical sensations, emotions) but it is not imperative that they fill it out in detail.

Some clients may struggle to name the emotions at first and may use words like 'uncomfortable'. In this case, use their own words and encourage them to explore the physical feelings in their body to help develop awareness of, and language for, their emotional experiences. For example, one client who was having experiences that sounded like anxiety, i.e. increased heart rate, breathing and racing thoughts, found it helpful to use the shorthand 'whizzy-ness' to describe this at first. We later explored this further, helping him understand more about anxiety and the associated thoughts, physical sensations and impulses.

MORE INFORMATION ON MANAGING UNWANTED BEHAVIOURS

Supplementary Handout: Procrastination and **Supplementary Handout:** Anger use the same approach for managing procrastination and problems with anger. The handouts provide information about these challenges and the common thoughts and emotional experiences. They formulate the unwanted behaviour as resulting from understandable challenges in managing the emotional experience and encourage both exposure to the emotion and learning to respond in more helpful ways. They both refer to **Core Handout:** Managing Emotions and Impulses. We usually start with the **core handout** and give the supplementary handouts alongside or afterwards if further information seems helpful.

In the case of anger, there is hyper arousal (fight or flight), and emotion regulation strategies are often focused on calming. Procrastination can be associated with a few emotional and physical states. Some people report hyper arousal and overwhelm and they may benefit from strategies to calm them so that feel able to approach the task. Others may describe *hypo* arousal, i.e. low motivation and fatigue. In fact, many clients report leaving things to the last minute as a way of increasing energy and motivation levels to help them think clearly and work effectively. They benefit from strategies to raise arousal levels to help them engage with the task at an earlier stage and then to keep themselves alert and engaged, for example moving or fidgeting, listening to uplifting music.

LINKING BACK TO THE FORMULATION

As you formulate the emotional experiences in the way described here, you will discover more elements of the 'here and now' experience that may need targeted support, and we describe them briefly here. Some coping behaviours can be considered in the context of the longitudinal formulation and can be addressed further later (Chapter 8).

Triggers

It helps to explore triggers (antecedents) of unwanted behaviours. When are angry outbursts most likely to happen? In what situations is the client likely to spend money without thinking it through? What sorts of tasks do they put off? You can then problem-solve with them how to manage the situation to reduce the likelihood of the unwanted behaviour.

For example, if spending impulsively, they could try using a pre-pay card or cash to limit spending money, writing a shopping list or going to shops with fewer temptations. Practical measures to limit screen time may help with compulsive scrolling or gaming.

The client may need further support. For example, someone who procrastinates may benefit from support from a manager to plan tasks that they put off, someone who spends impulsively may benefit from help from a partner to budget or someone who is having anger outbursts may need support with childcare to help when they are 'overloaded'.

Executive functioning and mood

It may be helpful to consider with the client the relationship between mood or emotion and executive functions and to include this in their formulation. For example, when discussing the Window of Tolerance concept, we explain that executive functions such as attention and flexibility work best when we are in the 'window'. Conversely, it is harder to withhold an impulsive response when already in an excited mood or to initiate a task they have put off when thinking about it makes them feel very anxious. So emotion regulation has two benefits: to help the client learn more helpful responses to ADHD challenges and to reduce the ADHD challenges themselves.

Thoughts and beliefs

You may notice thoughts that can be challenged in relation to the client's emotional responses. For example, relating to shame, there may be self-critical thoughts about their ability or value as a person or about what others think of them. Relating to anxiety, there may be thoughts about negative evaluation by others. This can lead to increased self-focus on attentional difficulties, which then worsen, leading to further negative appraisals and more anxiety. Some common thinking patterns in anger and procrastination are detailed in **Supplementary Handout**: Procrastination and **Supplementary Handout**: Anger. You may become aware of other factors such as perfectionism that can be explored in more detail (see Chapter 10 and **Supplementary Handout**: Perfectionism). You may become aware of themes in the client's thinking and of underlying beliefs that can be addressed later in therapy.

Chapter 7 summary

- Impulsive or unwanted behaviours often result from unhelpful ways of managing emotional experiences.

- We help clients understand their emotional experiences so they can learn how to respond in alternative, more helpful ways. This includes:
  - facts about emotions
  - information about action urges or impulses
  - using the Stop! Stay! Choose! Strategy to resist impulses.

- Formulation helps clients understand and address:
  - triggers to unwanted behaviours
  - thoughts and beliefs, such as self-criticism
  - the relationship between executive function and mood.

Beliefs and Coping

Handouts:

- **Core Handout:** Beliefs and Coping
- **Supplementary Handout:** Perfectionism

Once the therapist and client have a good, shared understanding of the links between automatic thoughts, emotions, physical reactions and behaviours, and there is progress towards therapy goals, it is time to explore in more detail long-standing patterns of thinking and responding. This will have been discussed to some extent in the assessment and the initial formulation.

It is now possible to develop a more detailed longitudinal formulation, identifying key core beliefs, rules for living and unhelpful compensatory strategies and their effects. Having recognized these, you can then help the client generate new, more helpful beliefs and behaviours and test them out. It is assumed that as a cognitive behavioural therapist you will know how to do this, so here we discuss identification and modification of underlying beliefs specifically with reference to ADHD-specific factors.

ADHD-related challenges result not only from the condition itself but also from *the understandable beliefs and compensatory strategies that follow.* The compensatory strategies in turn maintain those beliefs and exacerbate ADHD challenges, forming a vicious cycle. As the client recognizes this cycle, they see the possibility that ADHD challenges can be *managed*, as opposed to being fixed and beyond their control (as is often believed). It becomes clear that new self-beliefs and coping behaviours could change how ADHD challenges present, reduce their impact and so reduce distress.

CORE BELIEFS IN ADULT ADHD

Core beliefs result from experience, and growing up with a neurodevelopmental condition shapes experience in multiple ways. Neurodivergent people are at increased risk of adverse life events compared with neurotypical peers. They may have been through an education system that did not recognize or meet their needs, where their learning differences were misunderstood, even penalized. They may have had parents with mental health problems or who themselves were neurodivergent. (We do not suggest that having a neurodivergent parent necessarily leads to adversity. In some cases, it may be protective since a neurodivergent parent may be more aware of how best to support a neurodivergent child. However, a parent with their own unresolved challenges may find it harder to meet their child's needs.) Clients may have had less opportunity to access meaningful and positive work and other experiences, and they may have experienced stigma, rejection and criticism. Naturally, the common core beliefs reflect these experiences. See Table 3 for common core beliefs, rules for living and compensatory strategies in adult ADHD.

Table 3: Common core beliefs, rules for living and compensatory strategies in adult ADHD

Core beliefs	Rules for living	Compensatory behaviours
I am irresponsible I am unreliable I am unworthy I am lazy	Better not to try since I won't manage anyway I need to be exceptional to compensate for my lack of diligence	Keep expectations low, for example working in a role below one's ability, work for free or for low pay Work hard, 'overschedule', 'over-perform'
I am a failure I am not good enough I am inept I am stupid Others are critical	As long as I work hard and do things perfectly, I won't be found out In order to avoid criticism, I need to work extra hard I should always come across as competent I shouldn't admit defeat by asking for help	Try to get things 'just so', spend extra time, push oneself, don't take breaks Put things off, keep options open, don't finish things Worry Don't say no to requests, take on too much/overcommit ('people pleasing') Self-criticism Don't ask for help
I am different There is something wrong with me Others are rejecting	If people see the real me, I will be rejected	Hide or 'mask' ADHD challenges

My needs don't matter	I shouldn't ask for what I need	Don't assert own views, needs and wishes
	There is no point asking for what I need; even if I ask for what I need, I won't get it	Don't talk about feelings
		'Serve' others and prioritize others' needs at one's own expense
		Don't deal with things 'head on'
		Don't ask for help

As in other conditions, negative core beliefs may develop even without overtly abusive, critical or discriminatory experiences. The person may have compared themselves negatively with neurotypical siblings for whom certain things came more easily, perhaps developing the belief that they were not good enough. Other clients may have had a neurodivergent sibling with more challenging needs, which may have left the client's needs minimized or overlooked, leading to beliefs that their own needs do not matter or that others are unsupportive.

Negative core beliefs can develop at times of change. People with ADHD often report that challenges arise or increase after changes in education or work, moving away from home or the end of a relationship. Along with the other stressors inherent in life cycle transitions, there may be a move to a less structured environment or changes in expectations, for example independent learning at advanced stages of education. At the same time, there may be reduced support (from parents, a partner or the wider system), and the critical role this support had in keeping the person on track often only becomes apparent once it is no longer available.

What often emerges at these transitions is a discrepancy between the person's capability and putting it into practice. It may be that they have, until now, 'got by' without working hard or by completing things at the last minute. They may not have established consistent working habits or study skills or yet know what support is needed to meet their potential. The discrepancy between what they know they *can* do and what they *actually* do can cause frustration and distress and result in core beliefs such as 'I am lazy' or 'I am unreliable.'

While difficulties in education and the workplace in ADHD are common, they are not universal. In fact, many people are very able and successful *because of*, not despite, their ADHD, with strengths such as hyperfocus, creativity and high energy playing a key role in their success.

Here again, though, we may see perfectionism and beliefs that self-worth is contingent on achievement. Indeed, people sometimes develop negative core beliefs following praise or recognition for performing well. An emphasis on performance at the expense of other aspects of their life can lead to the conclusion that self-worth is contingent on external success and a core belief that they are unworthy.

Some people say that instead of negative core beliefs, they in fact have very positive ones – for example, that they are talented, can make persuasive arguments or can think on their feet to sort out difficult situations. It is possible to hold concurrent beliefs, and someone may be confident in the workplace but feel unworthy in their personal relationships and vice versa. It may be that the person has negative underlying beliefs but because they are abiding by their rules for living, they are not aware of them. As for anyone, it is only when the person risks breaking, or does break, these rules that negative core beliefs are activated (this is discussed further in the next section).

RULES FOR LIVING AND COMPENSATORY BEHAVIOURS

Rules for living are the 'intermediate' beliefs that help someone cope given the assumed 'truth' of the core belief. They are seen in the person's typical behaviours or 'compensatory strategies'. For example, someone with the core belief 'I am unreliable' may develop the rule 'Better not to try since I won't manage anyway' and keep expectations low, for example by staying in a job below their ability. They may avoid situations where they may be evaluated, for example by procrastinating (see Table 3 above).

We also see unrealistic expectations for work patterns based on what clients can do when they are hyperfocusing, expecting this level of work *all* the time. Executive functioning differences in planning can make it more likely that someone would set unrealistic standards. Because the standards are difficult if not impossible to meet, and perhaps compounded by executive functioning differences, it is common to then engage in compensatory strategies such as procrastination, maintaining a core belief that they are 'lazy', 'unreliable' or 'not good enough'.

Table 3 categorizes the beliefs into a few themes, for example, unreliability, failure, difference and that one's needs do not matter. Clinically, the most common compensatory strategies are procrastination, avoidance, setting overly high (perfectionistic) or low expectations, neglecting one's own needs, not being assertive, not asking for support and 'masking'. Masking (sometimes called 'camouflaging' or 'impression management') is the term for trying to hide ADHD symptoms to appear 'neurotypical' and to avoid negative evaluation.

This list of common beliefs and compensatory strategies is from anecdotal clinical experience rather than empirical study and is not exhaustive. In practice, there is considerable overlap between the compensatory strategies that are associated with the core belief themes. The important thing is to identify the client's idiosyncratic coping and the function of that behaviour for them. For one person, not saying no may have the function of avoiding criticism, while for another, it may stem from believing their needs do not matter (and for some, it may be both).

Core Handout: Beliefs and Coping explains the concepts of core beliefs and rules for living and illustrates them using Yemi as a case example. It then guides the client to identify their own rules for living and core beliefs.

SHAME AND SELF-CRITICISM

Bear in mind that clients may feel ashamed about or blame themselves for compensatory strategies. The process of exploring and understanding together how such strategies have developed is inherently de-shaming. Such coping will often have had a protective function, for example developing perfectionistic behaviours to avoid criticism. It helps to emphasize that we all do things for good reasons and that it is understandable, and was perhaps even inevitable, that they learned to cope in these ways.

Self-criticism and shame are countered by compassion. Through your therapist qualities of sensitivity, warmth and supportiveness, you will model compassion for the client and their past experiences. If possible, it helps to elicit and build the client's self-compassion by highlighting where they are being hard on themselves or blaming themselves for things that were not their fault and by encouraging more kindly self-talk. While we did not do this in the trial, in our general clinic practice, we have found it helpful to incorporate elements of Compassion Focused Therapy (Gilbert, 2010) if there is marked self-criticism.

DEVELOPING NEW BELIEFS AND BEHAVIOURS

Having developed the formulation, you can draw on the toolkit of CBT cognitive change methods including data logs, continuum methods, behavioural experiments and Thought Records (e.g. for self-critical thoughts) to develop and test new beliefs and coping behaviours. Note that in **Core Handout:** Beliefs and Coping the new rules for living are below the new core belief to be consistent with the layout of Worksheet: Identifying Core Beliefs and Rules for Living; however, as in all CBT, we develop new rules before new core beliefs.

As you identify new rules for living and coping behaviours, you can link these to therapy goals.

> For example, one of Yemi's goals was related to procrastination, i.e. she wanted to finish her reports before the deadline. She realized her belief 'I need to be brilliant to compensate for being unreliable' was related to unhelpful coping such as working long hours, over-performing, getting caught in the detail and procrastinating because her exacting standards made it hard to get started. So, in addition to building helpful habits and skills to help her plan and stay on task, *recognizing and challenging beliefs that had led to unhelpful coping* was key to helping her sustain new habits and skills.

This stage of Stage 2: Active Therapy provides an opportunity to explore changes in the individual's relationship with their ADHD, including an awareness of how their own or others' views of ADHD may have previously affected their self-beliefs. Beliefs about needing to be fixed or not being good enough may make way for self-acceptance and an appreciation of strengths and qualities.

> Yemi realized that her differences that had led her to believe she was worse than others were in fact unique and valuable things about herself. For example, she realized that, working in a team, her tendency to focus on the details was a great strength and complemented the abilities of other team members. In turn, she realized she could seek support to help her with the parts of the work that she found more challenging.
>
> We explored how Yemi's experiences had contributed to her high expectations for herself and her beliefs about others' expectations for her. We thought about how these beliefs had shaped her coping. Yemi reflected that not only had she expected unrealistically high standards

for herself, but she had also believed she needed to hide her ADHD challenges as well as her opinions and feelings. Recognizing these beliefs and coping behaviours and where they came from helped her find new coping behaviours that were more aligned with her values – for example allowing herself to make mistakes, to seek help and to express her views and emotions. This helped her to feel more confident and content with who she was and how she related to others.

Chapter 8 summary

- ADHD-related challenges result from not only the condition itself but also the understandable beliefs and coping behaviours that follow.
- This chapter described common ADHD core beliefs, rules for living and compensatory strategies.
- It illustrated ways of helping clients identify and challenge their beliefs and develop new, more helpful coping behaviours.

CHAPTER 9

Ending Therapy and Looking Ahead

We now describe the closing stage of therapy, Stage 3: Ending Therapy and Looking Ahead. The aims are to reflect on the therapy process and the learning and changes that have taken place as well as to prepare the client for the 12-week period before the follow-up, and final, session.

Handout:

- **Core Handout**: Ending Therapy and Looking Ahead

In the trial we planned a 12-week break between the end of therapy and the follow-up session (42 weeks after baseline assessment) to test whether therapeutic gains were maintained following the end of therapy (30 weeks after baseline assessment). The main outcomes were measured at the 42-week point. Our results showed that gains were maintained, and on some outcome measures results even slightly improved, compared with the 30-week point (Dittner *et al.*, 2018).

A central intention of CBT for adult ADHD is to help people understand their ADHD challenges so they can manage for themselves. So, if your service model allows, a follow-up period can be a helpful way for clients to test out how to keep new habits going once they are not attending regular sessions. Part of preparing for ending is helping them think about 'self-therapy' and about further support, either formal or informal. The following box presents a summary of the topics covered in these final sessions. These are described in more detail in this chapter.

SESSION 14

- Discuss ending therapy including client's thoughts and emotions about nearing the end of CBT.
- Review progress towards therapy goals and any remaining issues.

Homework: Look at and, if possible, complete the Therapy Summary in **Core Handout**: Ending Therapy and Looking Ahead before session 15.

Handout:

- **Core Handout**: Ending Therapy and Looking Ahead.

SESSION 15

- Review and, if not completed already, complete the Therapy Summary.
- Re-rate therapy goals.
- Identify targets for the next 12 weeks.

Homework: Self-management, e.g. regular diary appointments or discussions with a supporter to review goals.

SESSION 16: FOLLOW-UP AT 12 WEEKS

- Review the 12 weeks since the end of therapy.
- Review homework.
- Identify what is going well and areas of difficulty. Address any additional difficulties that have arisen, referring to the formulation as needed.
- Identify any practical steps to maintain therapeutic changes.
- Briefly assess the need for further support and make recommendations.
- Re-rate therapy goals.

SESSIONS 14 AND 15

We discuss the client's thoughts and emotions about ending therapy. In session 14, we review progress towards therapy goals and whether there are remaining issues (usually from the range agreed at the start of therapy) that the client would like to focus on.

As for other client groups, responses to ending therapy vary. You will have explained at assessment that therapy sessions are limited in number and that an aim of CBT is to help the client learn skills to manage independently. Some will feel confident about implementing what they have learned, perhaps even relieved to finish regular sessions, while others may want to continue therapy to manage their challenges. When clients lack confidence about ending, it helps to remind them about therapy aims. Discuss the coping strategies the client has in place and the support available outside of therapy; in some cases, this may include professional support. If it becomes clear earlier in therapy that ending will be difficult, then it helps to discuss it in earlier sessions. Uncomfortable or painful feelings such as loss can be anticipated, identified, normalized and validated.

Core Handout: Ending Therapy and Looking Ahead covers topics for this last therapy stage. It includes a written Therapy Summary for the client to complete. This, together with the rest of the handouts used in therapy (including their goals, targets and formulations), forms a Therapy Record that the client can refer to in the future.

The client may complete the Therapy Summary for session 14 homework and bring it to session 15 for discussion. Some clients will prefer to complete this with you in session 15. The Therapy Summary includes what they have learned about their ADHD challenges, advantages of ADHD, how ADHD challenges developed and what kept them going, any new beliefs and coping behaviours, things they would like to continue to work on, warning signs that challenges may be getting worse again and what they can do to make things better.

Discuss how the client will continue to manage their challenges and maintain any changes after therapy has finished. Consider with the client how they will know if setbacks have occurred and what to do in these instances. Many clients find it helpful to schedule 'self-therapy' appointments with themselves or with a supporter to review how things are going. It is helpful to explore with the client how they can use their Therapy Record (e.g. complete target sheets, carry out behavioural experiments or reflect on challenges in the context of their formulations), where they will keep it and how often they will check in with themselves or a supporter. Encourage them to consider seeking appropriate support in the future, either socially, at work or in education, or, if needed, professional support.

Ask the client to re-rate the goals they set at the start of therapy. Reflect on and positively reinforce all changes made and consider with them things they could try next. Where changes are not as the client may have hoped, reflect on this and help them consider the reasons, which may include life events or other barriers. Help them notice and address perfectionism and self-criticism. It helps to explain that goals are a tool to establish intentions and guide action and they are not 'a stick to beat yourself with'. Remind them it is not just about what they have done but also their experience of the process and what they have learned along the way. As well as changes in the challenges, highlight any differences in how they relate to them, the ADHD and how they think about themselves. Encourage the client to notice, and share your own observations, as to what they have brought to the process, for example their creativity, reflectivity, commitment, humour, resilience and persistence.

SESSION 16

In the final session consider with the client how they have found the 12 weeks without therapy – what has worked well and what has been more challenging? If they have forgotten about goals or targets or dropped habits, help them think about how to get back on track with self-compassion. Now is a good time to remind them that CBT has been about learning how to set goals and get back on track, dropping or changing habits is normal and the important thing is to notice and 'steer back on course'. Ask them to re-rate the goals they set at the outset of therapy. Explore with them how they intend to manage their ADHD challenges in the future, including practical steps such as self-therapy sessions and seeking additional support, and, if needed, assess the need for further input and make recommendations. Seek their final reflections on the process and their learning, add your closing reflections and say goodbye.

Chapter 9 summary

In the Stage 3: Ending Therapy and Looking Ahead sessions we:

- discuss ending therapy
- review progress towards therapy goals
- help clients develop a Therapy Summary
- support them in making plans to manage after therapy has ended.

CHAPTER 10

Additional Challenges and Therapeutic Considerations

ADHD is a diverse condition that impacts on multiple areas of life. This is reflected in the range of challenges that people with ADHD report and want to work on in their CBT. There may also be barriers or blocks to making progress in CBT. This chapter considers some of the common concerns, challenges or blocks that may arise, with suggestions on how to manage them, including the parts of the book that may be most helpful and where to find additional support. In Chapter 12, we provide some further reading and helpful resources.

THERAPIST FACTORS WHEN WORKING WITH ADHD

Many therapists say they lack confidence in working with this client group. However, we hope it has become clear through reading this book that, as a cognitive behavioural therapist, you already have the fundamental skills to work effectively with this group. Furthermore, many of the approaches and adaptations described are doubtless similar to those you already use with clients with other conditions.

In CBT the therapeutic relationship is fundamental to change (Beck *et al.*, 1979). The relationship can be defined through both generic alliance factors, such as warmth and positive regard, and elements that are specific to CBT and that directly facilitate cognitive and behavioural change, namely collaborative empiricism and Socratic dialogue (Kazantzis, Dattilio and Dobson, 2017). We are not aware of research evidence about the therapeutic relationship in CBT in ADHD specifically, but effective therapeutic relationships are those where the therapist adapts those relational elements to the client's needs, such as the degree and type of empathy to facilitate engagement (Dobson and Kazantzis, 2023).

In our clinical experience, this is no different in ADHD, i.e. it is important to balance generic skills of supportiveness and understanding with CBT-specific change techniques, while paying close attention and responding to the client's individual needs. These include their understanding of their condition, therapy goals, emotional state, levels of motivation and readiness for change.

There is good evidence that early symptom improvement in CBT is associated with better subsequent ratings of the therapeutic alliance. Therefore, it is important to help support the client to make changes as early as possible, to build confidence in the CBT approach and the therapeutic relationship. We know from research that behavioural change is a key ingredient of effective psychological therapies in adult ADHD. A key skill in this client group is thus to introduce such change in a way that is consistent enough to establish and embed new habits (using structure, homework tasks, repetition), whilst being flexible in how you do this and adapting to the client's style.

In supervision it may help to attend to client and therapist beliefs about the therapy. Clients may come to therapy with high expectations or ambitious goals, and therapists may feel under pressure to respond to these, setting up unrealistic expectations for therapy on both sides. We have found it helps to start small and experiment with modest changes at first. Therapists may also find themselves responding to the client's experiences of unmet need or marginalization. This may result in therapist behaviours such as 'going over and above' what they might do for other clients, for example typing up detailed therapy summaries to send after the session or allowing extra session time.

Therapists report finding it hard to know what is a *'reasonable'* adjustment, for example how flexible to be about usual therapy expectations such as timekeeping or how much to help the client with keeping a Therapy Record. In our experience, it is important to be clear and firm about the therapist and service expectations, whilst demonstrating understanding as to how ADHD challenges may get in the way and supporting them with those. In the example in Chapter 2 about helping the client get to sessions on time, we would gently explain that service demands mean we must stop at a certain time and ask how we can support them to start on time (rather than going over time at the end). When generating Therapy Records, we think with the client about how they can take their own notes or how to generate shared documents during the session rather than the therapist doing 'extra' outside of the session time.

Having explicit discussions about the therapeutic process can be helpful. This can start from the assessment when the therapist asks about previous experiences of therapy, more general help or support received, as well as about expectations. It is also important to discuss the therapeutic relationship in supervision, including how both the client's and therapist's beliefs may be impacting on the therapy process.

We are not aware of any research regarding therapists who are themselves neurodivergent working with ADHD. However, anecdotally, therapists' lived experience can enrich the therapeutic alliance and therapeutic process in ADHD. At the same time, it is not necessary to be neurodivergent to work effectively with neurodivergent clients. In our experience, for CBT with ADHD, as with any condition, the essential therapist qualities are openness, curiosity, willingness to learn and a commitment to collaborative empiricism.

As in other conditions, if the therapist has lived experience, judicious self-disclosure may be helpful for the client, though there is little research on therapist self-disclosure in CBT. It is important to use supervision to consider issues such as whether and how to discuss therapist neurodivergence with the client, as well as the rationale for doing so, to ensure that the client's needs are at the forefront of such decisions.

Anecdotally, neurodivergent therapists report that the added cognitive load of having to actively support the client's executive functioning can be challenging, for example when adhering to session structure. This need not be a barrier to delivering effective therapy and again can be supported using supervision.

ADHD AND IDENTITY
Responses to ADHD diagnosis

In the same way that there may be varied responses to other diagnoses, clients may respond to their ADHD diagnoses in different ways. It helps to be curious about their experience, allow time and space for them to talk about it and validate their responses. Relief, anger and grief are all possible responses; mixed feelings are common. Thoughts and feelings about the diagnosis often change over time.

Responses to the diagnosis reported in therapy vary depending on factors such as age at diagnosis (child versus adult) and length of time since diagnosis (recent versus long-standing). For instance, people who were diagnosed as children may have developed beliefs about being different from their peers, for example because of having to attend medical appointments and take medication or because of behavioural difficulties when they were younger. Beliefs about being different also develop in clients who were diagnosed later and can potentially be even more challenging, as they have had less understanding about the cause. Late or recently diagnosed clients can report feeling let down that others did not notice or provide them with suitable support when it was needed, for example during education. We can explore the potential reasons for this, i.e. we can recognize that health professionals' and public understanding of the condition has changed and that others were acting on the information that they had at the time, often with the best of intentions. While we cannot 'turn back time', we can acknowledge and validate the impact of these experiences.

Stigma, masking and disclosure

Many individuals are unsure whether to tell people about their ADHD diagnosis. This may be due to the stigma or discrimination still associated with neurodevelopmental conditions or for other reasons. As you explore this with clients, it helps to consider that this is not an 'all or nothing' decision; they can take their time and consider who they want to disclose to, what they want to share, why and when. Many clients find it helpful to discuss with their therapist the pros and cons of sharing and of not sharing.

If there are beliefs about stigma and difference, it is helpful to include them in the formulation and explore how these are related to the individual's coping behaviours (Chapter 8). Consider whether they are 'masking' (sometimes called 'camouflaging' or 'impression management'), i.e. trying to hide their symptoms to appear 'neurotypical' and to avoid feared negative evaluation with different types of behavioural and emotional suppression. This is commonly reported by clients during CBT, though research on ADHD masking is limited. In our clinical experience, while beneficial in some situations, if used to excess and as a compensatory strategy for negative self-beliefs, masking can form part of a self-perpetuating cycle that leads to further challenges. These include burnout, low self-esteem, mood problems and feeling disconnected from others, as well as the worsening of central ADHD challenges such as difficulty concentrating. We can help clients identify what masking behaviours are present and where – for example, are they in social situations, with certain types of relationships or in work settings? We can help them consider whether they are helpful or unhelpful – this is different for everyone and depends on context.

Learning to acknowledge, accept and express their feelings and cultivating more general self-acceptance and self-compassion will help the client to manage distress and to feel more confident. If they decide to 'drop the mask' or disclose their ADHD diagnosis, behavioural experiments can be a useful tool to test out negative expectations. It helps to explore how they can do this gradually, for example by dropping the mask in 'safe' situations or sharing their diagnosis with close friends at first and gradually sharing or unmasking in other settings with more people if, or when, they feel comfortable to do so. Some feel proud of their ADHD identity and choose an outright declaration and celebration of their neurodivergence.

There is no right or wrong amount to disclose or unmask – it is about finding the right balance of safety and authenticity for the individual. Whether or not people unmask entirely, many find it helpful to develop a peer support network of neurodivergent friends or join a support group with whom they can share the strengths and challenges of ADHD. Chapter 12 provides information about ADHD organizations.

Sex, gender and gender identity

Though sex and gender are distinct concepts, in previous ADHD research the terms have tended to be used interchangeably. Sex, gender and gender identity are likely to affect how the client experiences their ADHD. ADHD was historically thought of as a 'male' condition. The result was that research and clinical reports included more males than females (defined by the biological sex ascribed at birth) and the understanding of the condition was in turn shaped by how male participants behaved and thought.

ADHD is less likely to be diagnosed in females than in males, particularly in childhood. Females typically receive the diagnosis later and are less likely to be prescribed ADHD medication (Martin, 2024). More research is needed to ascertain reasons for this. Suggested possibilities include biological reasons (e.g. genetic factors leading to increased likelihood of ADHD in males), diagnostic practices (symptom descriptions may be more appropriate for identifying ADHD behaviours and difficulties in males than females or there may be a higher threshold for ADHD diagnosis in females compared with males) and socio-cultural factors (e.g. sex differences in presentation and compensatory behaviours). Regarding presentation, for example, it has been suggested that women are more likely to have inattentive rather than combined or hyperactive-impulsive subtypes, and because these symptoms are less disruptive to others than hyperactive-impulsive ones, they are less readily recognized.

The effect is that, compared to males, females are more likely not to have received recognition or support when it was needed. Studies suggest living undiagnosed until adulthood can have lasting negative impacts on self-esteem, mental health and overall wellbeing (Attoe and Climie, 2023). It can be helpful for the therapist to consider with the client how such factors may have contributed to the client's experience and to include them in the formulation.

Research shows that there are elevated rates of neurodevelopmental conditions like ADHD in people identifying as transgender or gender diverse (Warrier *et al.*, 2020). We are not aware of research that investigates whether transgender and gender-diverse individuals are more likely to be diagnosed later than cisgender individuals. However, it is helpful to consider that transgender and gender-diverse individuals have experienced marginalization and high rates of additional challenges including mental health challenges (Winter *et al.*, 2016). Again, when co-constructing their formulation, it is helpful to explore with the client how intersectional inequalities may have contributed to their experiences around ADHD and their distress.

Race, ethnicity and culture

In a similar way to the biases seen in sex and gender, ADHD research and clinical reports are biased with respect to race, ethnicity and culture, with the focus having been largely on Western/European countries and with predominantly White populations. There is therefore a lack of awareness and knowledge of how ADHD may present across different cultures and ethnicities, and this is reflected in inequalities in rates of diagnostic assessment and treatment. A US birth cohort found that Asian, Black and Hispanic children were significantly less likely to be diagnosed than White children and that White children were more likely to receive treatment for ADHD (Shi *et al.*, 2021). A smaller UK study found that most children and young people diagnosed with ADHD were from White British and White other backgrounds, with a relatively small proportion from Asian and Black backgrounds (Banerjee *et al.*, 2024).

There is also concern that unconscious bias may play a role in diagnostic decision-making and that behaviours seen in ADHD may be evaluated differently based on race or ethnicity. Several US studies have found that young people from African American and Hispanic backgrounds are more likely than their White counterparts to be given a diagnosis of disruptive behaviour disorder rather than ADHD (Fadus *et al.*, 2020). More research is needed on biases in ADHD diagnosis and treatment in relation to race and ethnicity in the UK. These factors can limit access to treatment and support and perpetuate societal injustice.

In addition to systemic factors, it is important to consider cultural barriers to diagnosis. Awareness, and indeed the concept, of neurodivergence varies across racial, ethnic and cultural groups. In some groups where there is less awareness or acceptance of the construct of ADHD, for example, a child's behaviour could be viewed by parents or their community as being disrespectful rather than resulting from neurodivergence, and they would therefore be less likely to seek support from services (Ofori, 2024). In some cultures, differing attitudes to mental health and health seeking and fear of stigma may deter people and their families from seeking support (Slobodin and Masalha, 2020; Faugno *et al.*, 2024). Both delayed diagnosis and stigma are known to be associated with negative impacts on mental health and ADHD treatment outcomes (Mueller *et al.*, 2012; Harpin *et al.*, 2016).

Becoming culturally competent neuro-affirmative therapists requires us to educate ourselves as to the intersections between neurodivergence and race, culture and ethnicity. It is essential to be curious so that our clients can share their culture with us and we can explore alongside them how these experiences have contributed to their challenges.

COMMON THINKING STYLES IN ADHD
Perfectionism

Since people with ADHD often struggle with organization and getting things done, it may seem surprising that many report perfectionism. Research into cognitions in adult ADHD found that perfectionism is the most commonly endorsed thinking bias (Strohmeier *et al.*, 2016). People with ADHD may be predisposed to perfectionism, 'all or nothing' thinking styles and difficulties tolerating uncertainty. Perfectionistic coping can also result from difficult life experiences.

Perfectionism can impact on therapy in several ways. First, it can affect setting goals and working towards behavioural targets. Clients may report negative automatic thoughts (NATs) such as 'I should be able to do this already' and 'It is pathetic that I have to learn this.' They may have unrealistic expectations of what they *should* be able to do and find it hard to identify or 'settle for' more modest targets or goals. Perfectionism may underlie 'boom and bust' behaviours and procrastination.

Consider perfectionism in the formulation, its relation to the client's challenges and the thoughts, emotions, physical reactions and behaviours that result. As you develop the longitudinal formulation, perfectionism may feature in the rules for living and compensatory strategies. **Supplementary Handout:** Procrastination can help the client understand more about the ways in which perfectionism can present and some ways to address it, which include behavioural experiments and challenging self-critical thoughts. For more information see *Overcoming Perfectionism: A Self-Help Guide Using Scientifically Supported Cognitive Behavioural Techniques* (2nd edition) by Roz Shafran, Sarah Egan and Tracy Wade (2018). Building self-compassion can help in addressing excessively high standards and critical self-evaluation. More on using self-compassion as a therapeutic technique can be found at www.compassionatemind.co.uk and in *Compassion Focused Therapy: Distinctive Features* by Paul Gilbert (2010).

Cognitive rigidity

Cognitive rigidity is common in neurodevelopmental conditions, including ADHD, and stems from executive functioning differences. It leads to difficulty taking different perspectives, introducing change and considering alternative options, all processes that, of course, are inherent to CBT. If cognitive rigidity is impacting on therapy, one option is to concentrate on behavioural change rather than cognitive change processes.

If you engage in cognitive change work, it may be easier to look at the processes of thinking rather than the content. Through Socratic questioning, explore with the client the differences between 'all or nothing' thinking styles and 'both/and' thinking (that is the idea that multiple things can be true at the same time and that there can be multiple ways of thinking and feeling about a situation). It can help to explore with the client the pros and cons of thinking in a particular way rather than challenging it directly.

It can also help to provide some information about executive functioning differences. Emotional states impact on executive functioning, so it will be more difficult to be cognitively flexible at times of increased stress and high emotion. Knowing this can help some clients to notice their thinking styles and find more adaptive ways of coping. For example, one client noticed that when he was under pressure at work, he would become more 'tunnel visioned', i.e. finding it hard to take alternative perspectives. This led to 'perseverative' working habits (overworking) and expressing impatience with colleagues. Recognizing these patterns allowed him to take steps to reduce his stress levels which in turn made it easier to generate alternative perspectives and responses.

SOCIAL RELATIONSHIPS
Social skills

ADHD can affect relationships in various ways. First, people may report social skills challenges such as interrupting conversations, using blunt language, being 'overbearing', 'oversharing' or not noticing their impact on others. There is an overlap between ADHD and autism traits, so these challenges may, for some, come from a difficulty in understanding social rules and others' mental states. However, many people do understand these things but challenges stem from self-regulation, i.e. managing behaviour, emotions and attention in social situations. At assessment, you can ask about this: 'Some people say they find social situations difficult because they don't understand the "unspoken rules"; others say they know what to do or say but that the ADHD challenges [relate to client's stated challenges, e.g. impulsivity] get in the way – what do you think makes social situations hard for you?'

Your formulation will identify the client's idiosyncratic social challenges and, from this, ways to manage differently. Recognizing and managing emotional experiences in social settings may help to manage impulsive behaviours such as talking instead of listening and cracking jokes at inappropriate times. You may help the client learn and practise communication skills, for example assertiveness skills for those who find it hard to get their needs met or to manage conflict. This is covered in **Supplementary Handout**: Anger. There is further information on social skills in *ADHD in Adults: A Psychological Guide to Practice* by Susan Young and Jessica Bramham (2006).

Rejection sensitive dysphoria

Many people with ADHD use the term 'rejection sensitive dysphoria' or 'RSD' to describe their social challenges. This is not a diagnostic term or one of the formal ADHD diagnostic criteria, and there is limited research into the condition; however, it is a term used widely in ADHD communities and by some health professionals. As the name suggests, it refers to heightened sensitivity to criticism or rejection. It has cognitive, emotional, physical and behavioural components and as such can be readily formulated and addressed using a CBT framework. Clinical characteristics of RSD are as follows:

Cognitive. Self-critical thinking, negative self-talk, cognitive biases leading to a negative or critical interpretation of others' behaviour, rumination and worry.

Behavioural (compensatory strategies and safety-seeking behaviours). Behaviours focused on avoiding rejection or criticism including withdrawal and avoidance, people pleasing behaviours, overworking and perfectionism.

Emotional. Intense emotional responses, such as crying or anger, to perceived rejection or criticism, feelings of shame.

As in other forms of distress, the understandable coping responses inadvertently exacerbate the problem and maintain negative self-beliefs; people with RSD are frequently distressed by social relationships or avoid them altogether. Emotion regulation difficulties and a tendency to experience emotions intensely are also likely to contribute to the emotional responses. Your formulation will allow you and the client to identify and address the idiosyncratic factors maintaining their challenges and distress. The managing emotions, NATs and underlying beliefs and behaviours sections of Stage 2: Active Therapy can all be used to manage these experiences.

Impact of ADHD

ADHD challenges can impact on relationships in other ways. For example, financial difficulties can take a toll on relationships (see later in this chapter for more information). Spouses or family members can find themselves providing additional support or taking on an unequal load to compensate for organizational challenges. It can be hard for loved ones to know how best to support and how much responsibility to take on. If there are stressful conflicts resulting from the ADHD challenges, family and systemic therapy may be indicated, as this can help the couple or family understand and work through the challenges together. Support groups are available for ADHD adults and their supporters.

Adult carers may be entitled to social care support. The first step is to get an assessment (a carer's assessment) from the local authority adult social services department, who will decide whether the carer's needs meet the eligibility criteria and prepare a support plan of eligible needs. Further information is available here: www.nhs.uk/conditions/social-care-and-support-guide/support-and-benefits-for-carers/carer-assessments.

WORK AND EDUCATION

Adults with ADHD in the UK are protected by the Equality Act which makes it unlawful to discriminate against someone because of a disability. Further information is available here: www.gov.uk/guidance/equality-act-2010-guidance.

Education providers and employers have a legal obligation to make reasonable adjustments for disabled people, including those with ADHD. These changes could include having a desk in a quiet area and help in organizing their work. It is not necessary to have a diagnosis to meet the definition of disabled – the definition relates to how the condition affects the person rather than what the condition is.

Further information on how to ask for reasonable adjustments in work and education is available from the websites of the following organizations:

- Scope is a UK disability charity: www.scope.org.uk.
- ADHD UK is a UK charity for those affected by ADHD: https://adhduk.co.uk.

Access to Work

Adults with ADHD in the UK who are in work, self-employed or about to start work may be entitled to fully funded support (such as coaching) from the government disability scheme known as Access to Work. People with ADHD can receive support if they are (1) disabled (Equality Act 2010, includes ADHD) or have a health condition that impacts their ability to work, (2) aged 16 or over and (3) live in Great Britain.

The support provided will depend on their needs. They can apply for a grant to help pay for practical support with their work, support with managing their mental health at work and money to pay for communication support at job interviews. More information can be found on the government website: www.gov.uk/access-to-work and through ADHD UK: https://adhduk.co.uk/access-to-work.

Students
Most college or university settings will have disability support services that can help think about reasonable adjustments and resources such as workshops to support with study skills. Students with ADHD may be eligible for Disabled Students' Allowance (DSA) funding to help cover study-related costs.

Information about how to apply and eligibility criteria is available on the government website: www.gov.uk/disabled-students-allowance-dsa.

FINANCIAL PROBLEMS
ADHD can lead to financial problems due to problems at work, impulsive spending, gambling or disorganization. In the ADHD community the term 'ADHD tax' is sometimes used for financial loss incurred as a direct result of the condition, for instance from forgetting to pay bills, not reading terms and conditions, missing flights, losing possessions and so on. (It can also refer to the extra mental effort and resources that they must put into tasks compared with those without the condition.) Some of the following strategies may help in managing finances:

- Setting up automatic payments such as direct debits for recurring bills.
- Planning spending/budgeting – some bank accounts help allocate money to different pots.
- Using calendar alerts for financial deadlines.

Information about managing finances and benefits can be provided by the following organizations:

Citizens Advice. A charity that provides free advice and support on various issues including benefits, debt and money: www.citizensadvice.org.uk.

MoneyHelper. A government-backed website providing free and impartial money and pensions guidance: www.moneyhelper.org.uk.
Scope. A charity that campaigns for equality and fairness for disabled people. Their website contains advice and support on many issues including money and finances: www.scope.org.uk/advice-and-support/money-and-finances.

BEHAVIOURAL ADDICTIONS – GAMING AND GAMBLING

Unwanted or unhelpful behaviours in ADHD may reach the level of a behavioural addiction that needs support in its own right. These include gaming and gambling, for which specific CBT therapy protocols have been developed. For more information see the National Centre for Gaming Disorders: www.cnwl.nhs.uk/national-centre-gaming-disorders and the National Gambling clinic: www.cnwl.nhs.uk/services/addictions/national-gambling-clinic.

ADHD MEDICATIONS

NICE guidelines (National Institute for Health and Care Excellence, 2018) recommend medications as the first-line treatment and non-pharmacological treatment for adults with ADHD who have made an informed choice not to take medication, have difficulty adhering to medication or have found medication to be ineffective or cannot tolerate it, or where they have benefited from medication but still have significant ADHD symptoms. First-line medications are stimulant based (lisdexamfetamine and methylphenidate); non-stimulant medications (such as atomoxetine) can be used if they are not effective or cannot be tolerated.

Clients' choices around medication use and their experiences vary. In our clinical experience, some report clear improvements after starting medication and cite it as a key factor in their readiness for psychological therapy. For some, it is less straightforward; for example, they may initially be excited when starting medication but become disappointed as it becomes clear that some problems will not remit with medication alone. Others feel strongly that they do not want to take medication and want to learn ways of managing their condition without it.

If your client is taking ADHD medication and has any questions or concerns, it is important that they discuss these with the clinician responsible for prescribing their medication (their GP or ADHD specialist). Following this, CBT techniques may be helpful in managing common side effects such as insomnia. Clients may also find it helpful to think in CBT sessions about strategies to help remember to take their medication.

There is limited research about medication use and CBT efficacy. Our trial did not control for medication use but did include both those who were and those who were not taking medication. Only a few studies have compared the efficacy of CBT with and without medication. One study of a CBT group therapy with and without medication found that those on medication showed greater improvements compared with those without, though the superiority decreased over the follow-up period as the CBT-only group continued to improve (Cherkasova *et al.*, 2016). Two studies have found that CBT leads to significant improvements to ADHD symptoms, functioning and emotional outcomes with and without medication (Weiss, 2012; Pan *et al.*, 2019).

CHAPTER 11

Summary and Conclusions

We have described individually tailored, formulation-driven CBT for ADHD. This book is based on the manual from a randomized controlled trial that we carried out to evaluate this intervention and that found it to be efficacious.

The CBT described here aims to target the specific beliefs and behaviours that worsen both the ADHD challenges themselves and the associated distress. We have described the three stages of therapy – Stage 1: Assessment and Therapy Planning, Stage 2: Active Therapy and Stage 3: Ending Therapy and Looking Ahead.

Our neuro-affirmative approach helps the client to see their ADHD characteristics as differences not deficits and seeks to support rather than correct these differences. Throughout, we have emphasized the importance of a warm and supportive therapeutic alliance and the need to actively address the shame and self-criticism that are common in this client group. We have described a collaborative approach whereby the client and therapist work alongside each other to discover how ADHD-related challenges have developed and worsened, with the aim of helping the client to feel understood and accepted and empowering them to cope.

As we end, we pay tribute to the participants in the trial and clients we have met through research and routine clinical practice. Their insights, openness and commitment to the research and the therapeutic process have helped us shape our thinking about ADHD and CBT and the information that we share in this book, and we hope this will help many others. We close with some quotes from trial participants:

> I can't concentrate for longer, but I can bring myself back when I go off task. The main thing that has helped is not to try to fight the way my mind works. If I take little breaks, some longer breaks and a lunch break

I can achieve more. Using a to-do list and being vocal with colleagues [about challenges and support needed] has helped a lot.

I know why I get angry now. I can be more accepting and less harsh with myself about it, which makes it easier for me to look after myself. I can stay calm and express dissatisfaction earlier and in more helpful ways.

I still lose my keys – but my perspective has changed. I am more forgiving and empathic [with myself]; I feel more confident.

CHAPTER 12

Further Information and Resources

All information is correct at the time of writing.

ADHD DIAGNOSIS AND TREATMENT

The NHS website contains information about diagnosis, symptoms and treatment: www.nhs.uk/conditions/attention-deficit-hyperactivity-disorder-adhd.

Royal College of Psychiatrists – ADHD in adults: www.rcpsych.ac.uk/mental-health/problems-disorders/adhd-in-adults.

ADHD CHARITIES AND ORGANIZATIONS

ADHD Foundation works in partnership with individuals, families, doctors, teachers and other agencies to improve emotional wellbeing, educational attainment, behaviour and life chances through better understanding and self-management of ADHD, autism and related learning difficulties: www.adhdfoundation.org.uk.

ADDISS provides people-friendly information and resources about ADHD for parents, people with ADHD, teachers or health professionals: www.addiss.co.uk.

ADHDadultUK is a charity for adults with ADHD, run by adults with ADHD. It provides peer-led support and coaching to adults with ADHD to support multiple aspects of living with ADHD: www.adhdadult.uk.

ADHD Aware runs peer support group meetings for ADHD adults, their partners and parents of ADHD young adults: https://adhdaware.org.uk/adhd-support-group-meetings.

ADHD UK is a charity founded in 2020, with a mission to help those affected by ADHD – either those who have ADHD or those close to them: family, friends, employers and co-workers: https://adhduk.co.uk/about-us.

INFORMATION ABOUT OTHER NEURODEVELOPMENTAL CONDITIONS
Autism
National Autistic Society: www.autism.org.uk.

The NHS website: www.nhs.uk/conditions/autism.

Autism and mental health
Royal College of Psychiatrists: www.rcpsych.ac.uk/mental-health/mental-illnesses-and-mental-health-problems/autism-and-mental-health.

Dyslexia and dyscalculia
The NHS website contains information about dyslexia symptoms, diagnosis and management: www.nhs.uk/conditions/dyslexia.

British Dyslexia Association has information about dyslexia and dyscalculia including assessment: www.bdadyslexia.org.uk.

Dyspraxia – also known as developmental co-ordination disorder
The NHS website contains information about developmental co-ordination disorder symptoms, diagnosis and management: www.nhs.uk/conditions/developmental-coordination-disorder-dyspraxia.

FURTHER READING ON CBT AND ADULT ADHD
The following publications include more information about ADHD and some helpful CBT strategies:

Ramsay, J. R. and Rostain, A. L. (2015) *The Adult ADHD Tool Kit: Using CBT to Facilitate Coping Inside and Out.* New York: Routledge.

Ramsay, J. R. (2024) *The Adult ADHD and Anxiety Workbook.* Oakland, CA: New Harbinger Publications.

Safren, S. A., Sprich, S. E., Perlman, C. A. and Otto, M. W. (2017) *Mastering Your Adult ADHD: A Cognitive-Behavioral Treatment Program: Therapist Guide.* New York: Oxford University Press.

Young, S. and Bramham, J. (2012) *Cognitive-Behavioural Therapy for ADHD in Adolescents and Adults: A Psychological Guide to Practice.* Chichester: Wiley-Blackwell.

FURTHER READING ON CBT

Beck, J. S. (2020) *Cognitive Behavior Therapy: Basics and Beyond* (3rd ed.). New York: Guilford Press.

Fennell, M. J. V. (2016) *Overcoming Low Self-Esteem: A Self-Help Guide Using Cognitive Behavioral Techniques.* London: Robinson.

Greenberger, D. and Padesky, C. A. (2016) *Mind over Mood: Change How You Feel by Changing the Way You Think* (2nd ed.). New York: Guilford Press.

McKay, M. and Fanning, P. (2016) *Self-Esteem.* Oakland, CA: New Harbinger Publications.

Core and Supplementary Handouts

Core Handout: CBT and Adult ADHD

Supplementary Handout: Activity Diaries

Supplementary Handout: Managing Distractions

Supplementary Handout: Time Management

Core Handout: Thinking Patterns in ADHD

Core Handout: Managing Emotions and Impulses

Supplementary Handout: Procrastination

Supplementary Handout: Anger

Core Handout: Beliefs and Coping

Supplementary Handout: Perfectionism

Core Handout: Ending Therapy and Looking Ahead

All handouts in Appendix 1 and 2 can be downloaded as PDFs from https://digitalhub.jkp.com/redeem using the code QLFCSKE.

CORE HANDOUT: CBT AND ADULT ADHD
What is adult ADHD?

Attention Deficit Hyperactivity Disorder (ADHD) is a clinical diagnosis used to describe a set of characteristics that include:

- inattention, e.g. difficulty concentrating, missing important details
- hyperactivity, e.g. being constantly on the go, restless, agitated
- impulsivity, e.g. acting without thinking enough first.

The characteristics are present from childhood and, for some, continue into adult life. In relation to the ADHD diagnosis, these are called 'core symptoms'. People with symptoms in all these domains are diagnosed with 'ADHD combined subtype'. Those with attention differences only are diagnosed with 'ADHD inattentive subtype'. Finally, people with hyperactivity and impulsivity only are diagnosed with 'ADHD hyperactive-impulsive subtype'.

Not everyone with these characteristics will experience them as problematic or to the extent that they feel they need diagnosis or support.

Different ways of viewing ADHD

ADHD is a clinical diagnosis and as such this is the language we use. However, this is just one of a few 'lenses' we can use to view this set of characteristics. The lenses do not exclude each other. At the same time, we can view ADHD characteristics through a 'social disability' lens – that is, that people are disabled by barriers in society rather than their 'impairment' or difference. We take a *neuro-affirmative approach*. We also view ADHD through the *'neurodiversity* lens', that is, as one of the many ways in which human beings naturally vary. We value and support those variations and appreciate ADHD as a difference, not a deficit.

People with ADHD typically seek CBT for support in managing challenges associated with their ADHD. People relate to their ADHD in different ways, and there are no 'right' ways to think or feel about it, or to respond to it. We aim to help you explore how ADHD has affected, and continues to affect, you and to support you in making life as good as it can be, in the ways that you choose.

ADHD characteristics

ADHD is an 'umbrella' term that includes a variety of characteristics and therefore affects people in different ways. It may lead to challenges in multitasking, forgetting things, getting distracted, finding it difficult to start and complete tasks (procrastination), losing one's temper or not being able to sit still or stop spending money. People with ADHD have differences in 'executive functioning' or the 'control centre' of the brain. These are brain functions concerned with organization, planning, holding things in mind and regulating behaviour and emotion.

What causes ADHD?

ADHD is thought to result from a combination of biological, psychological and social (bio-psycho-social) factors. There is evidence that genes may play a role, as many people with ADHD have a close relative with a similar condition. There is also evidence that a difficult family life or childhood trauma can increase the risk of developing ADHD. Other factors that have been suggested, such as watching TV, playing computer games or diet, have not been found to be related to ADHD.

Having ADHD can be tough – it impacts on education, work and relationships, it makes day-to-day tasks more challenging and people often report feeling criticized or misunderstood. Perhaps unsurprisingly, people with ADHD are more likely to have a mental health problem such as depression or anxiety.

It is important to remember there are advantages and disadvantages to every characteristic: alongside the challenges of the condition, people with ADHD talk about enjoyable characteristics such as being fun-loving, spontaneous and creative.

Are there any aspects of your ADHD that you enjoy? Do you experience any advantages to your ADHD? What are they?

A way forward

We do not choose the characteristics we are born with. Furthermore, we do not choose our experiences which result from the environments that we grow up in. So the important thing is not to blame ourselves – or others – for current difficulties but to think about how to cope helpfully now. This booklet and your CBT are designed to help you do this by helping you learn about your challenges and try new ways to manage them.

A CBT approach to understanding ADHD

CBT stands for cognitive behavioural therapy. 'Cognitive' means thinking, reasoning and remembering. An important part of CBT is to understand links between cognitions, behaviours and feelings. CBT is therapy that helps us change how we *think* and *behave* so that we *feel* better.

First, CBT for adult ADHD can help in managing the core ADHD characteristics (or symptoms) of inattention, hyperactivity and impulsivity. However, the challenges in ADHD also relate to the experience of growing up with and living with the condition. They include additional challenges of stress, anxiety, low mood, low self-esteem, relationship difficulties or anger. CBT can help with these too.

Your therapy will be tailored to your needs. The first step to helping you manage your ADHD is to understand where challenges came from and how they affect you now.

Factors that contribute to ADHD challenges: predispositions and experiences

CBT considers the bio-psycho-social factors that contribute to ADHD and then keep it going. Let's first consider the factors that contribute.

We are predisposed to be a certain way through biological (e.g. genetic, physical health) factors. In the case of ADHD, someone may be predisposed to be energetic or sensitive or find it difficult to concentrate – in the CBT diagram in Image A1 there is a box for this called 'predispositions'.

The environment and our experiences (psychological and social factors) then shape how those predispositions develop. For example, sporting talent is a predisposition, but intensive training and support (experience) is needed to become a successful sportsperson. In a similar way, we all need to be taught and to practise skills such as organization, planning and self-management. Due to our predispositions, some of us may need more help and support than others. Negative experiences or a lack of support may also make it harder for someone to develop their potential. In Image A1 there is a box called 'experiences'.

Factors that can worsen ADHD challenges: thoughts and behaviours

If someone does not get the support they need or has negative experiences, such as criticism for being disruptive or not paying attention, they are less likely to learn and practise effective coping strategies, such as organization and planning. They may instead learn unhelpful coping habits, such as avoidance and procrastination. In this way, a predisposition can become shaped by the person's experiences into a common way of coping or responding. They are likely to develop negative thoughts about their ability which will affect how they feel and what they do. The thought 'I can't do it' might lead to feeling anxious and avoiding a task. In this case, the person does not learn whether they could do it and they do not learn helpful coping. This is one of the ways thoughts and behaviours can worsen ADHD challenges.

Image A1 shows how these factors could feed into core ADHD challenges such as inattention, hyperactivity and impulsivity as well as ADHD-related difficulties such as anxiety.

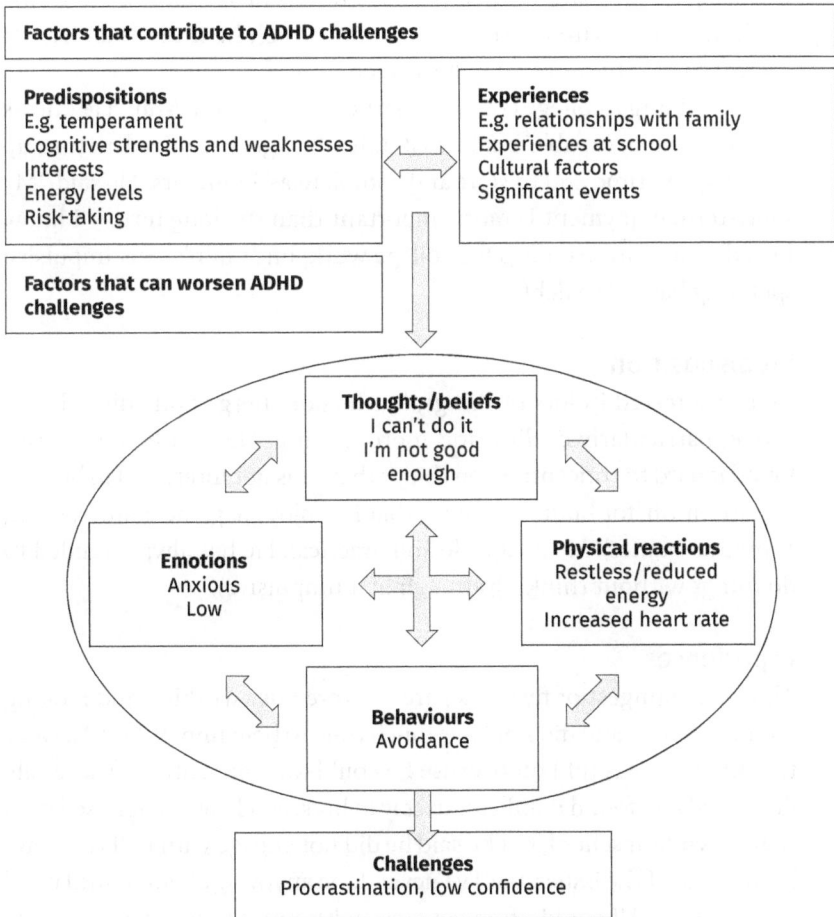

Image A1: Example factors that contribute to and worsen ADHD challenges

Case example: Ali

Ali is a fictional client, but we hope that you might find his story helpful as an example of how CBT can be a tool to support Ali in making the changes he would like. We will return to his story in later handouts.

Ali is a 20-year-old man who was diagnosed with ADHD when he was nine years old. He lives with his parents. At the CBT assessment, Ali said that his main difficulties were organization, starting and completing college assignments and impulsive spending.

Strengths and challenges

Ali is currently working in a technical, practical job which he enjoys, and he gets good feedback for his work. He thinks he is more suited to the 'shop floor' compared with written work which he finds 'tedious' but wants to study to move on in his career.

Ali is doing a college course as part of an apprenticeship. He knows he is 'more than capable' but finds it difficult to get organized, to turn up to college on time and to start and complete assignments. He said, 'My short-term enjoyment is more important than the long term – I know I need to use my evenings for college work, but I don't.' His impulsive spending has led to debt.

Predisposition

Ali is interested in lots of things, has lots of energy and enjoys being active, particularly cycling and motorcycling. He said he has always found it hard to concentrate on things that he is not interested in but can pay attention 'for hours' to things that he enjoys (e.g. mechanics, bikes, computer games). He is capable and practical. He has always tended to do things without thinking enough first (impulsive).

Experiences

Ali is the youngest of five. His parents were busy working and looking after the family and did not have much time to help him. When Ali went to school, he was told off because he could not concentrate, was easily distracted and found it difficult to stay in his seat. He was diagnosed with ADHD while at school, but he said he did not engage with it: 'I've always been aware of the issues, but I've never done anything about it until now.'

At school Ali could often get away with not doing much work. He said, 'When I was doing my GCSEs, I knew I wasn't bothering but I didn't need to.' As a result, he did not learn how to organize his work or develop good study habits. He said his parents tried to advise him, but he ignored their comments.

When he started A levels, things 'went downhill'. He struggled with concentration, planning and doing the work, so he decided to leave college early and get a job.

Thoughts and beliefs

Ali said he often has thoughts like 'I deserve to have some fun' which lead him to do things he enjoys instead of his work. When he thinks about work, he has thoughts such as 'I can't do it' and, after putting off work or spending money, 'I can't control myself' and 'I'm a failure.'

Emotions

Ali often feels anxious and sometimes frustrated.

Physical reactions

When Ali feels anxious, he finds it more difficult to settle down to start a task or to stick with it. Sometimes he wants to get up and move, and other times he is drained of energy. At these times, his attention and concentration are worse than usual.

Behaviours

When Ali has college work to do and feels anxious, he often ignores the work and 'moves on immediately' to more interesting things such as cycling, going online and gaming. He can 'hyperfocus' on these for hours and said he does not know how to 'pull away' and refocus on what he needs to do, i.e. his college work. Recently he has been spending money without thinking enough first.

Ali's difficulties are summarized in Image A2.

Factors that contribute to ADHD challenges

Predispositions
If interested can concentrate for hours; if not interested won't pay attention at all
Capable, good at practical tasks
High energy, enjoy being active
Impulsive

Experiences
Big family: parents busy
Told off at school, felt criticized
Compared self to friends who found things easier
Diagnosed ADHD in childhood, 'did not engage' with it
Did not build organization and study habits
Left college early

Factors that can worsen ADHD challenges

Thoughts/beliefs
I can't do it
I am never going to be able to do this
I deserve to have fun
I'm a failure

Emotions
Nervous, anxious, frustrated

Physical reactions
Want to move, full of energy and 'can't settle', sometimes drained
Concentration worse

Behaviours
Ignore what I need to do, 'move on immediately' and do something else
Spend money without thinking enough first

Challenges
Disorganization, leave things to the last minute (procrastination), impulsive spending and debt, lack of confidence

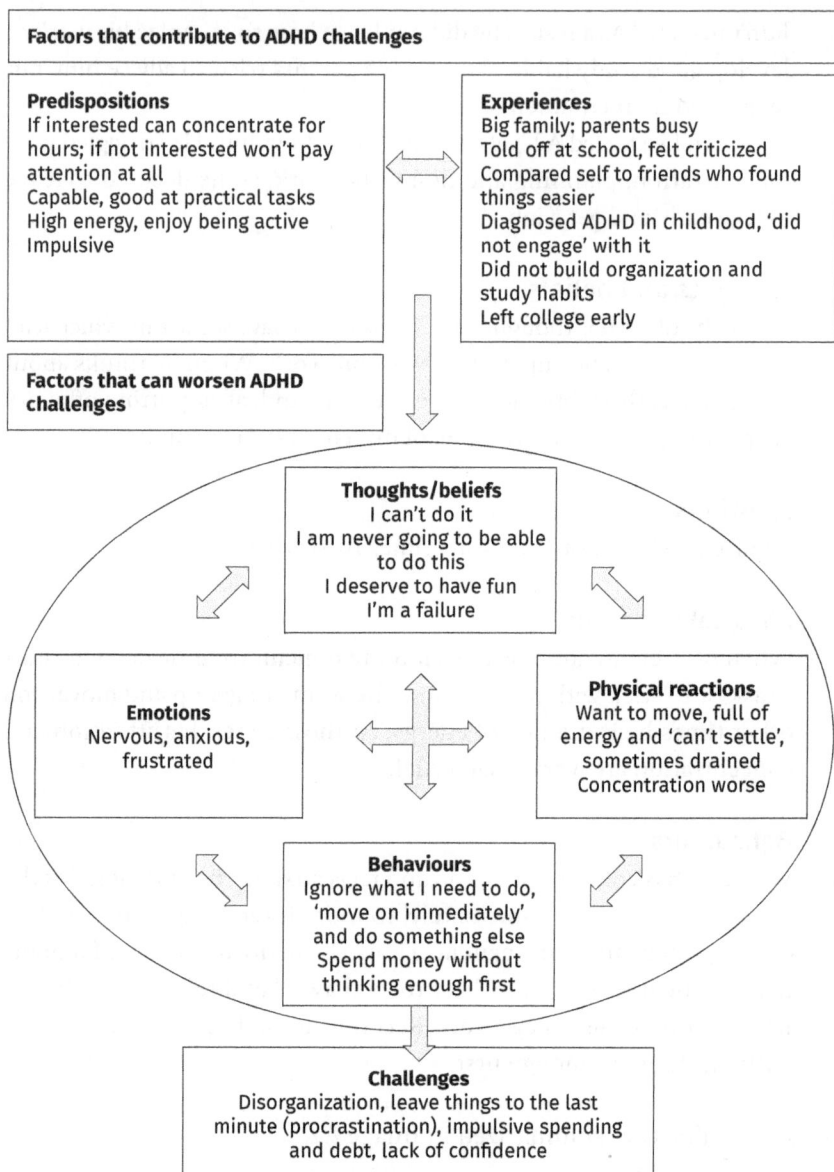

Image A2: Factors that contribute to and worsen Ali's ADHD challenges

Ali has created a 'map' of his ADHD with the help of his therapist. You can use the blank diagram in Image A3 to map the factors involved in your ADHD. Your therapist can help with this. You might like to make a start on your own and continue to work on this in a session with your therapist.

Factors that contribute to ADHD challenges

Predispositions

Experiences

Factors that can worsen ADHD challenges

Thoughts/beliefs

Emotions

Physical reactions

Behaviours

Challenges

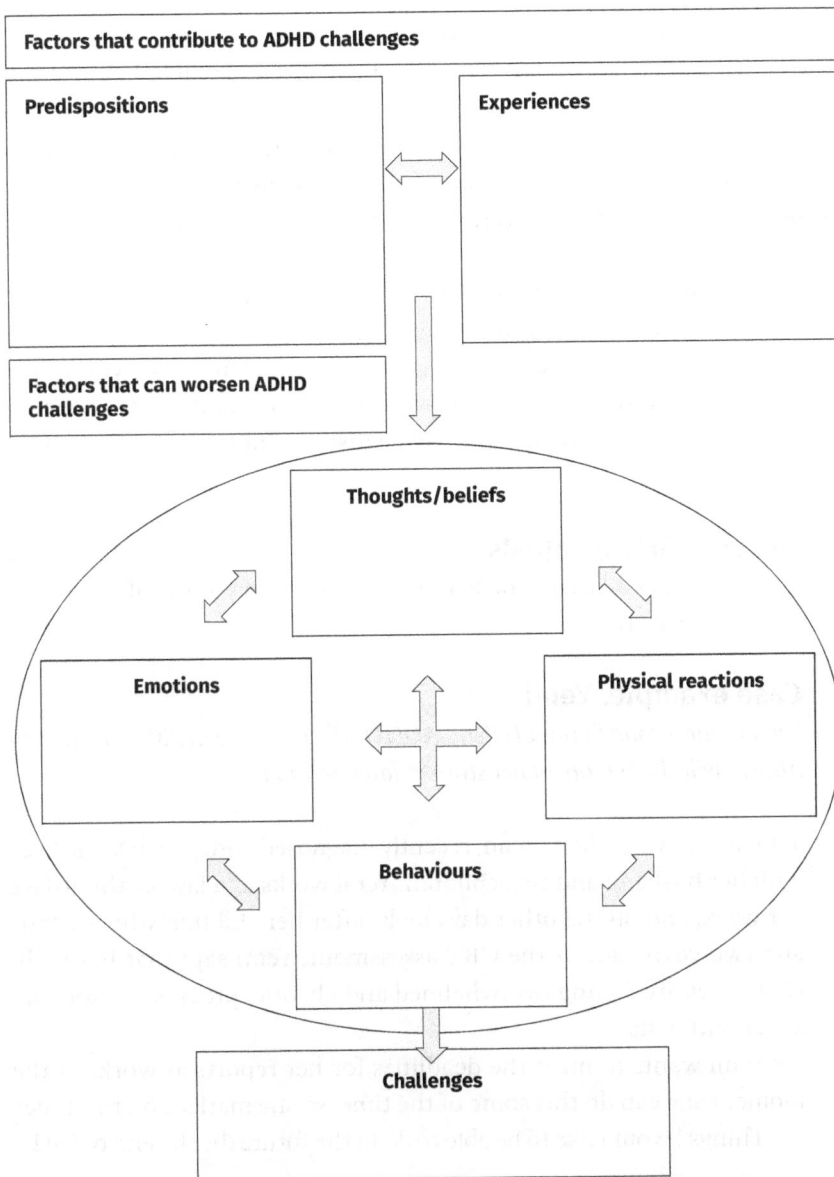

Image A3: Factors that contribute to and worsen my ADHD challenges

What will CBT involve?

CBT is a practical therapy, so you and your therapist will start by identifying your personal therapy goals. These will be specific to you and
the things you want to do in your life. It is not about 'making' you
do anything that you do not want to do or find to be important. For

example, not everyone with ADHD wants to work on time management. Your CBT will be tailored to your specific needs and will help you work towards your own goals.

Usually, in the early stages, we will work on targets or steps towards your goals. These may be helping you to remember appointments or improving organization. Later, we will explore how unhelpful patterns of thinking and coping have developed and help you try new ways to manage these. You will find that the different areas in the map of your ADHD will be addressed at different stages of therapy.

Each week, you and your therapist will agree things for you to try between sessions to work towards your goals. This may include keeping a diary, trying out strategies to manage distractibility or making a note of thoughts.

Identifying therapy goals

We can use a scale like the one below to write down your goals and your progress towards them.

Case example: Yemi

Yemi is our second fictional client. ADHD affects her life in different ways to Ali. We will share more of her story in later handouts.

Yemi is a 41-year-old woman, recently diagnosed with ADHD. She lives with her husband and two children. Yemi works as a lawyer three days per week, and on the other days looks after her children who are four and two years old. At the CBT assessment, Yemi said that her main challenges are feeling overwhelmed and chaotic, procrastination and anger outbursts.

Yemi wants to meet the deadlines for her reports at work. At the moment she can do this some of the time, so she marks 2 on the scale:

Things I would like to be able to do in the future (by the end of CBT):

I. Complete all reports the day before the deadline
    At the moment I can do this:

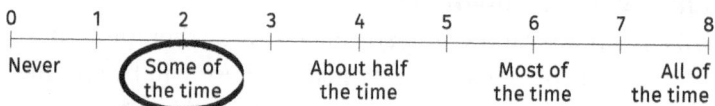

```
0        1        2        3        4        5        6        7        8
|--------|--------|--------|--------|--------|--------|--------|--------|
Never          Some of          About half        Most of          All of
               the time         the time          the time         the time
```

You can use the following worksheet to record your therapy goals.

WORKSHEET: IDENTIFYING THERAPY GOALS

Date: . . . .

Things I would like to be able to do in the future (by the end of CBT):

1. . . . .

At the moment I can do this:

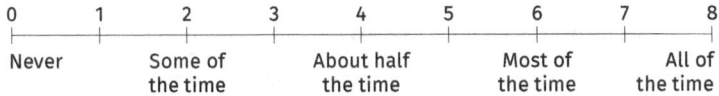

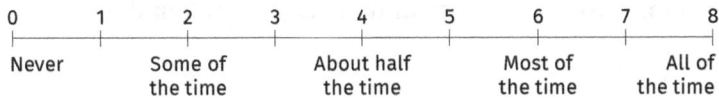

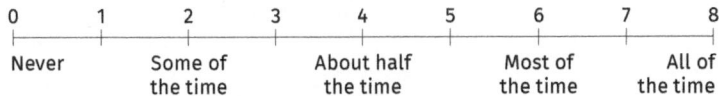

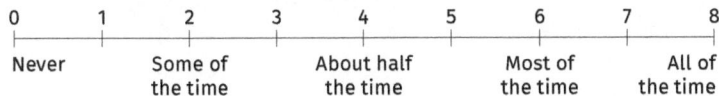

0	1	2	3	4	5	6	7	8
Never		Some of the time		About half the time		Most of the time		All of the time

2. . . . .

At the moment I can do this:

0	1	2	3	4	5	6	7	8
Never		Some of the time		About half the time		Most of the time		All of the time

3. . . . .

At the moment I can do this:

0	1	2	3	4	5	6	7	8
Never		Some of the time		About half the time		Most of the time		All of the time

4. . . . .

At the moment I can do this:

0	1	2	3	4	5	6	7	8
Never		Some of the time		About half the time		Most of the time		All of the time

WORKING TOWARDS YOUR GOALS

By breaking goals down into steps, you can try new things one step at a time.

For example, if your goal is to remember all appointments, these steps may be:

Step 1	Buy a diary
Step 2	Keep it in a particular place
Step 3	Write appointments in the diary as soon as they are made
Step 4	Look in the diary at least once per day
Step 5	Check the diary before making any other commitments and add those too

You can use the following worksheet to break down your own goals into steps.

You may like to make a list using the format in the worksheet or, if you are a more visual person, to draw a diagram or 'mind map'.

WORKSHEET: BREAKING THERAPY GOALS INTO STEPS

Goal 1: ....

Step 1	
Step 2	
Step 3	
Step 4	
Step 5	

Goal 2: ....

Step 1	
Step 2	
Step 3	
Step 4	
Step 5	

Goal 3: ....

Step 1	
Step 2	
Step 3	
Step 4	
Step 5	

Goal 4: ....

Step 1	
Step 2	
Step 3	
Step 4	
Step 5	

Setting up a personal reward system

Research shows that people with ADHD are more motivated by small, frequent rewards than by bigger, longer-term ones compared with people without the condition. This can lead to doing fun or interesting things while forgetting about time or consequences.

At the same time, people with ADHD often tell us they do not reward themselves or plan enjoyable activities. Sometimes they say they cannot enjoy downtime. They feel guilty taking time for themselves when there are things left undone or avoided or think they do not deserve to enjoy themselves. People may miss out on enjoyable activities because they find it hard to plan or deliberately not plan enjoyable activities in case they need to make up 'wasted time'.

As well as not rewarding themselves or missing out, many people also believe that criticizing themselves will motivate them to achieve more. In fact, the opposite is true – criticism (whether from yourself or others) is likely to discourage you. Instead, we know from psychological research that frequent praise and reward provide the most powerful motivation. You can use this knowledge to your advantage to help motivate you and help you stay on track.

The following worksheet is a space to record the rewards and enjoyable activities that motivate you. You can add to this list throughout therapy.

WORKSHEET: REWARDS AND ENJOYABLE ACTIVITIES

It is helpful to write a list of rewards so that they are there when you need them. Try to include a range:

Daily rewards

These are things you can easily do throughout the day and are not so absorbing that they take you off track. For example, drinking a cup of tea, listening to a song or doing a puzzle.

1. . . . .

2. . . . .

3. . . . .

4. . . . .

5. . . . .

Weekly rewards

These are things you may do regularly – once or more per week. They are more time-consuming than the daily rewards and add interest and pleasure to your life. For example, playing sport, creative activities such as knitting or playing an instrument and social activities such as meeting a friend for a drink.

1. . . . .

2. . . . .

3. . . . .

4. . . . .

5. . . . .

Occasional rewards

These are 'treats', such as going to a concert, spa or sports event, that may be expensive or need more planning.

1. . . . .

2. . . . .

3. . . . .

4. . . . .

5. . . . .

Things that help you start tasks or stay on track

These may be things that energize you to get started, for example listening to uplifting music, or keep you focused, for example working alongside someone else ('body doubling').

1. . . . .

2. . . . .

3. . . . .

4. . . . .

5. . . . .

CBT TO SUPPORT ADULTS WITH ADHD

Recording what you do

Once you have agreed what you will try between each session, you can record this using the Therapy Record Form. There is space to record the date of the next session and topics to discuss at the next session. You can also write down the rewards and enjoyable activities planned for that week.

Ali's example Therapy Record Form

Session 1   **Date:** 1/12

Before the next session I will work on the following therapy goal(s):

- Do college work in the evenings

The next step(s) is/are:

- Do 30 minutes of college work Monday, Tuesday and Wednesday evenings

Write these targets in the space below and mark in the box every day that you manage them:

Targets	Mon	Tue	Wed	Thurs	Fri	Sat	Sun	Mon	Tue	Wed	Thurs	Fri	Sat	Sun
Do 30 minutes of college work Monday, Tuesday and Wednesday evenings														

Before the next session I will also:

- Read **Core Handout:** Thinking Patterns in ADHD

Rewards and enjoyable activities (what and when):

- Gaming in the evenings after 30 minutes of college work
- Cycle ride at the weekend

Next session date: 8/12

Next session I would like to talk about:

- Mind wandering when trying to do college work

Therapy Record form

Session number: ....   Date: ....

Before the next session I will work on the following therapy goal(s):

....

The next step(s) is/are:

....

Write these targets in the space below and mark in the box every day that you manage them:

Targets	Mon	Tue	Wed	Thurs	Fri	Sat	Sun	Mon	Tue	Wed	Thurs	Fri	Sat	Sun
....														
....														
....														

Before the next session I will also:

....

....

....

....

Rewards and enjoyable activities (what and when):

....

....

....

....

Next session date:...........................

Next session I would like to talk about:

....

....

....

....

Reviewing and setting new targets

Every week, you and your therapist will review your targets. You may not always complete tasks and you may not get results straight away. During therapy, you may also have times where you do not manage things that you had managed before. This is normal: the important thing is to be kind to yourself and work out what happened and how you can get back on track.

It is up to you when to move on to the next steps towards your therapy goals. You may keep the targets the same for a week or two while you fine-tune them. As a rule, if you have met last week's targets between 50% and 75% of the time, then it may be time to try the next thing.

It is fine to review targets as you go and 'tweak' them so that they feel most helpful for you. For example, you may change jobs and need to get up at a different time. Try to acknowledge any achievements, however small they seem to you, as this will encourage you to carry on.

Handout summary

- CBT helps change how we think and behave so we feel better.
- It can help in managing core ADHD characteristics (such as attention) and additional challenges (such as anxiety).
- We can 'map' ADHD to understand how ways of thinking and coping have developed and made ADHD challenges worse.
- CBT is a practical therapy, and the first step is to identify goals, which your therapist will help you to work towards.

SUPPLEMENTARY HANDOUT: ACTIVITY DIARIES

Your therapist may suggest that you monitor what you do (activity) over a week or so.

An Activity Diary can give us an accurate picture of how you spend your time. It can, for example, help you notice where you are doing more or less than you would like. This is useful when working towards therapy goals such as reducing procrastination, managing your time or doing more things you enjoy.

Your therapist will agree with you how to use the diary, how to remember to do it and how to record what you do. This is a tool, so you can agree the best way to use it to gather the information that you need.

We suggest you just write a few words for each of the main things you did in each two-hour period.

Ali's completed Activity Diary

Week commencing: 3/4	Monday	Tuesday	Wednesday	Thursday	Friday	Saturday	Sunday
Hours asleep last night	8	6	7	7	7.5	6.5	9.75
6am–8am	Get up	Get up	Get up	Get up	Get up	Bed	Bed
8am–10am	Travel to work and start (20 minutes late)	Travel to work and start on time	Travel to work and start on time	Travel to work (25 minutes late)	Travel to work and start on time	Got up 9.30am	Got up 9.45am
10am–12pm	Work	Work	Work	Work	Work	Cycling Lunch	Shops
12pm–2pm	Lunch 12–12.30pm	Lunch 12–12.30pm	Lunch 12–12.30pm	Lunch 12–12.30pm	Lunch 12–12.30pm	Cycling	Worked on car
2pm–4pm	Work	Work	Work	Work	Work	Cycling	Lunch Worked on car
4pm–6pm	Work and travel home	Work and travel home	Work and travel home	Work and travel home	Work	Put off work Game	TV
6pm–8pm	Game	Game	Eat	Eat	Friend's house	Put off work Game	TV Eat
8pm–10pm	Game	Game	TV	TV	Friend's house	Put off work Game	Assignment
10pm–midnight	Game	Game	Online	TV Bed	Friend's house	Pub	TV Bed
Midnight–6am	Game until 12.30am Eat Bed	Bed	Bed	Bed	Friend's house	Bed	Bed
Time I went to sleep	1am	Midnight	Midnight	11.30pm	3am	Midnight	11pm

Activity Diary

Week commencing:	Monday	Tuesday	Wednesday	Thursday	Friday	Saturday	Sunday
Hours asleep last night							
6am–8am							
8am–10am							
10am–12pm							
12pm–2pm							
2pm–4pm							
4pm–6pm							
6pm–8pm							
8pm–10pm							
10pm–midnight							
Midnight–6am							
Time I went to sleep							

SUPPLEMENTARY HANDOUT: MANAGING DISTRACTIONS

Some of the following may help with attention. You can make a note of things you have tried already and things you would like to try.

Reducing distractions in your surroundings

	Tried already	Try
Workspace:		
Keep a tidy workspace		
Face desk away from distractions, for example a window or busy room		
Electronic devices:		
Limit access to your device: turn your phone over, use airplane mode or keep it in a different room		
Limit distractions while using your device: reduce the number of open tabs, minimize notifications or use 'do not disturb' settings		
Sounds:		
Reduce background noise, use headphones or earplugs		
Alternatively, add sound – this is highly personal, so experiment with the following:		
Music or spoken word radio/podcasts		
White, brown or pink noise – these are sounds of different frequency ranges, available to stream online		
Adjustments for additional sensory sensitivities:		
Light (bright lights or certain wavelengths)		
Temperature		
Touch (e.g. wearing soft, comfortable clothing)		

Of the reducing distractions techniques you have tried already, what has worked?

. . . .

. . . .

. . . .

Does anything get in the way of these things working? If so, what?

....

....

....

What would you like to try?

....

....

....

Using 'external' tools to support attention

If we try and keep too many things in mind at once, then we use valuable working memory to think of them when we are trying to concentrate on other things. For this reason, it helps to use 'external' tools to keep a note of, and to remind us to do, things.

	Tried already	Try
Write down and record:		
Use diaries, to-do lists, shopping lists, notes and voice notes		
Cues, prompts and reminders:		
Display signs and notes around the house, for example a note on the front door reminding you to take your keys		
Ask a family member or partner to remind you to do something, such as take medication or a break		
Electronic reminders and alarms on the phone, computer or smart speaker to prompt you to do something		
Reminders and alarms to interrupt 'hyperfocus' or remind you to get back on task when distracted		
Use a timer:		
Set for short intervals to bring back your attention when it wanders – start with small chunks and gradually increase the time as your concentration span improves		
Set a specific amount of time to complete a task – when the timer goes off, choose your reward from your reward list		
If you underestimate the time, note the estimated and actual task timings to learn how long things take		

Which of the tools you have tried already has worked?

. . . .

. . . .

. . . .

Does anything get in the way of these things working? If so, what?

. . . .

. . . .

. . . .

What would you like to try?

. . . .

. . . .

. . . .

Seeking support

- If you have a manager, they may be able to help with:
  - the job itself in the form of help with structuring time and workload
  - putting in place reasonable adjustments.
- If you are self-employed, it may be possible to access guidance via peer support or mentorship.
- Adults with ADHD in the UK who are in work, self-employed or about to start work may be entitled to fully funded support (such as coaching) from the government disability scheme known as Access to Work. More information can be found on the government website: www.gov.uk/access-to-work and through ADHD UK: https://adhduk.co.uk/access-to-work.
- Working alongside another person either in person or virtually, known as 'body doubling', can help people stay on task. ADHD support groups offer body doubling spaces on video calls, and there are also live streams online of people working.

SUPPLEMENTARY HANDOUT: TIME MANAGEMENT

Many people with ADHD have time management problems and report running late and missing appointments and deadlines. This can lead to feeling stressed and overwhelmed.

There are three main steps to effective time management:

- A diary or calendar to record appointments.
- A to-do list to capture all the things that need doing.
- A daily plan to help you decide when to do things.

This handout describes each in turn. These are just suggestions – you may not want to follow these approaches completely but instead use them as a starting point for discussions with your therapist and for experimenting with what works for you.

Many people say they know these principles but need help putting them into practice. This is covered later in this handout.

Using a diary

The best diary is the one you will use – there is no 'right' sort. It can be electronic or paper. They are most useful if you always keep them in the same place (usually with you) and if you use them in a consistent way. Use colour coding or icons to help organize the information.

If you need to keep track of other family members, then also use a family wall planner or calendar with a separate space for each person's activities. Put this where everyone can see it. Encourage the rest of the family to mark their own appointments and events as they arise. Make a note in your personal diary or ask people to message you so that you can check your schedule on the family calendar before committing. Electronic shared calendars are also available.

1. Add appointments (e.g. a social event) or deadlines (e.g. a project is due) in the diary. Try to do this immediately.

    If you do not have your diary with you, ask the person you are making the appointment with to message you with the details and then add it to the diary when you see the message.

2. Look at the diary at least once a day and ideally more often. The following tips may help:

- Always leave the book or device in the same place (by your bed, in your pocket/bag, etc.).
- Try to look at it before or after something else that you do every day, e.g. cleaning your teeth or eating your breakfast.
- Put a reminder on your phone or alerts in your electronic diary.
- If needed, ask someone to remind you or help with this every day.

3. Plan a time each week when you can look ahead in your diary (and /or family calendar) and plan for what is coming up, e.g. you may need to go shopping, buy a train ticket or plan a journey. Check messages for appointments and add these to the diary.

To-do lists

To-do lists capture in one place everything that you need or want to do. You may divide the lists into weekly and longer-term tasks and are likely to need separate ones for home and work. Create a new, dated, list each week so that you can clearly see what needs to be done. Add items to the list as they come up. Plan a regular time each week to write and review the list. (If you have a longer-term list, you may want to review this too and add items from here to the weekly list.) Again, colour coding and icons can help organize the information.

Daily plan

Your daily plan is made up of appointments in your diary and items from the to-do lists and helps you to prioritize tasks and allocate times.

Even if you use an electronic diary, you may find it helpful to write your daily plan on paper, at least the first few times. Many people say this helps their attention and memory and teaches them about their thinking processes. With practice it will become quicker.

1. Date the list.

2. Jot down everything that needs to be done, checking your personal diary (and family calendar if applicable) to include any existing appointments and the weekly to-do list for additional tasks.

3. Write the estimated time to complete it next to the activity. Be

generous and remember to factor in travel time and interruptions. You can also jot down other information such as location.

4. In addition to what needs to be done, think about what you would like to do if you have time.

To do Wednesday 3 July		
Dentist appointment (town centre)		30 minutes
Buy train tickets for Saturday		15 minutes
Pick up kids		1 hour
Tidy up		30 minutes
Exercise		Up to 30 minutes
Groceries (town centre)		30 minutes
	Milk	
	Bread	
	Batteries	
	Washing liquid	

Note: If it is short, you can include your shopping list on the daily plan.

Try to be realistic. Start with just a few items so that you can easily manage it all (even just one or two items). It will feel good to cross things off your plan when they are done, and this will encourage you to continue.

5. Prioritize – decide which things are most urgent today. Urgency is context specific: in the example below, tidying up is not marked as urgent, but it may become urgent if it is left for too long.
   - A is for the most urgent tasks that need to be done today or tomorrow.
   - B is for the less urgent tasks that need to be done in the longer term. Some portions of the task may be completed in the short term, but others will take longer.
   - C is for lowest urgency tasks – these may still be important but could be done at another time.
   For this strategy to work, either complete or schedule a time for all A items before moving on to Bs and Cs.

To do Wednesday 3 July		
A Dentist appointment		30 minutes
B Buy train tickets for Saturday		15 minutes
A Pick up kids		1 hour
C Tidy up		30 minutes
A Groceries		Up to 30 minutes
A Groceries		30 minutes
	Milk	
	Bread	
	Batteries	
	Washing liquid	

6. Choose an order – allocate the tasks to specific time slots. Some things will already have either a set time, such as appointments and going to work, or a rough time, such as meals and other routine activities.

To do Wednesday 3 July		
10.15–10.45am	A Dentist appointment	30 minutes
	Lunch	45 minutes
2.30–3.30pm	A Pick up kids	1 hour

Then slot the other items on your day list into the time that is left over. Allow time between tasks in case they take longer than expected, and when estimating journey times, allow time to pack what you need to take.

7. Breaks and rewards – plan these throughout the day. Think about how long you can concentrate/sit still for. For example, if you can manage 15 minutes in one go, then aim to have a break every 15 minutes.

   If possible, allow time for enjoyable and relaxing activities every day. Remember that people with ADHD are more motivated by small immediate rewards than by longer-term ones. If you find a task boring or difficult, plan something you enjoy immediately afterwards as a reward (e.g. the coffee and snack after the dentist). You can also plan enjoyable activities to do alongside some of the things on your list to help keep focus, for example listening to a podcast while tidying.

To do Wednesday 3 July			
10.00–10.15am	Walk to town		15 minutes
10.15–10.45am	**A** Dentist appointment		30 minutes
10.45–11.15am	**Reward:** coffee and snack		
11.15–11.45am	**A** Groceries		
		Milk	
		Bread	
		Batteries	
		Washing liquid	
11.45am–12.00pm	Walk home		45 minutes
12.15–12.30pm	**B** Buy train tickets for Saturday		15 minutes
12.30–1.30pm	Lunch		45 minutes
1.30–2.00pm	**C** Tidy up (listening to podcast)		30 minutes
2.00–2.30pm	**C** Exercise (listening to music)		30 minutes
2.30–3.30pm	**A** Pick up kids		1 hour

Keep the plan with you so you can refer to it and make changes as needed.

8. Review – at the end of the day, review your list and note undone or unfinished items on your weekly list so they can be carried over to another day.

Make a new daily plan every day instead of writing on old ones. Time taken to plan at the start of the day may save time later, helping you to get more done and feel calmer.

Blocks to time management

Below are some examples of things that get in the way. Your therapist can help you find ways of dealing with these.

Changes to the plan

Unexpected events may occur, things may take longer than you expect or priorities may change. When this happens, remember this is normal and you *have not made a mistake*. Try not to abandon your list; instead, adjust timings or swap tasks round to accommodate the change. Being flexible is part of successful time management.

Underestimating time

People with ADHD often underestimate how long things take, choosing the 'best case scenario' rather than accounting for the inevitable delays. Remember to allow time for missed or delayed public transport, bad traffic or meetings running over.

Knowing where to start

It is hard when a backlog has built up. If it is not clear where to start and if there is not an immediate deadline, then start anywhere – pick one or two things at random. You will feel a sense of achievement for ticking them off the list, and if there are any urgent items, they will soon become clear. The main thing is not to spend time overthinking it. If there are too many things for today or some longer-term projects, see the next section on longer-term goals.

Saying yes to everything (overcommitted)

- Look at your schedule before accepting new projects.
- If you no longer have time for something, if you can, talk to the people involved and explain.

- Get help with solving the problem – maybe someone else can do it or help you.
- Notice thoughts, e.g. about productivity or pleasing others.

Not sticking to the plan

Try to start again as soon as you notice. Congratulate yourself for noticing you stopped. Remind yourself with kindness that it takes time to start new habits and conscious effort to maintain them. The important thing is not to criticize yourself but to get back on track as soon as you can. Your therapist can help you address distractibility (difficulty staying on task) or hyperfocus (getting stuck on one task).

What stops time management working for you?

. . . .

. . . .

. . . .

What goes through your mind about this?

. . . .

. . . .

. . . .

What could you do differently or try out?

. . . .

. . . .

. . . .

Longer-term planning

If tasks have several steps or are parts of ongoing projects, you may find it helpful to have a separate list of things that need to be done over a period of several weeks and months. You can then add items from this list to your weekly list as necessary.

It can be difficult to know where to start with bigger projects, so it is helpful to think about how to break the task into manageable steps.

Breaking goals into steps

You can use a similar process to the one described in **Core Handout: CBT and Adult ADHD** to break down your task into steps. If you are a more visual person, you can use a diagram or mind map. Each of these steps can then become items on your daily or weekly to-do lists.

For example, if your goal is to paint a wall:

Step 1	Look at paint samples to choose colour
Step 2	Buy paint and brushes
Step 3	Prepare the space: • Move furniture • Put down dust sheets
Step 4	Paint
Step 5	Tidy up: • Clean brushes • Remove dust sheets • Put back furniture

There will be some 'trial and error' when breaking down the task into steps, and this is a normal part of the process. If you find you are getting stuck on a step, it may help to think about how to break it down further. In the example above, steps 3 and 5 can be broken down into more than one task.

CORE HANDOUT: THINKING PATTERNS IN ADHD

As you will have learned so far, experiences shape our thinking and behaviour. Our thinking and behaviour are also related to our emotions and physical reactions, and Image A4 illustrates how these elements are all linked.

Understanding this can help us to think and to respond differently. In turn, this may help manage challenges and related stress or distress.

Look at Image A4 below: each of the areas in the diagram influences all the other areas.

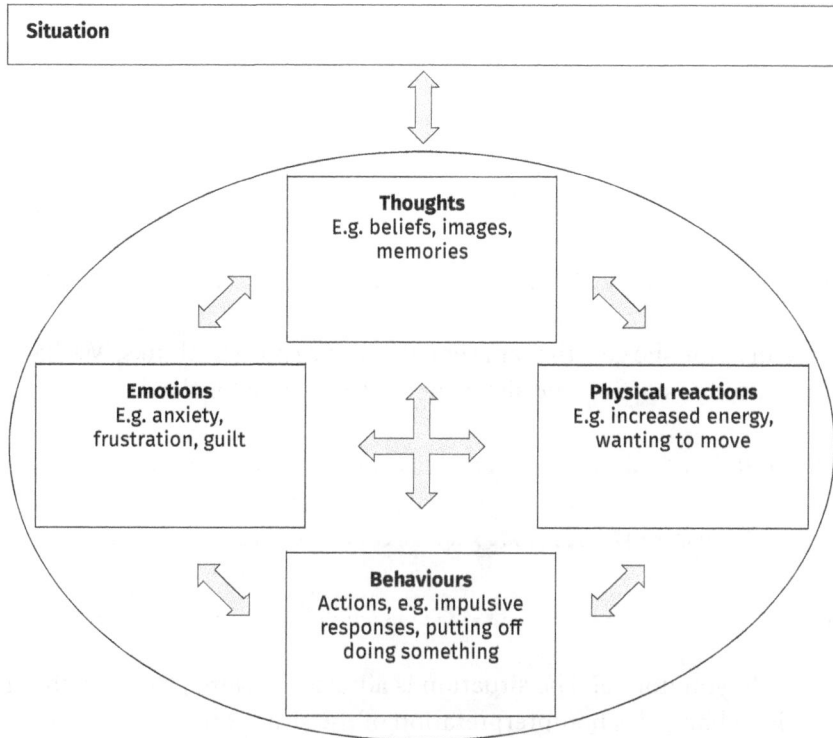

```
┌─────────────────────────────────────────────────────────┐
│ Situation                                                 │
└─────────────────────────────────────────────────────────┘
```

Thoughts
E.g. beliefs, images, memories

Emotions
E.g. anxiety, frustration, guilt

Physical reactions
E.g. increased energy, wanting to move

Behaviours
Actions, e.g. impulsive responses, putting off doing something

Image A4: The cognitive-behavioural five areas

For example:

If you complete an important piece of work on time (behaviour) you may feel happy (emotion) and are likely to think positively (thoughts) about your achievement.

If you drink a cup of coffee (behaviour) you may notice your heart rate increase (physical reaction) and you may feel more alert (physical reaction) and perhaps more anxious (emotion).

If you are late (behaviour), you may think, 'I should have organized myself better' or 'I am letting people down' (thoughts), and you may feel disappointed and cross with yourself (emotions).

The importance of the thought

How we think about a situation will influence our responses.

For example, imagine the following scenario: Yemi, our fictional client from **Core Handout**: CBT and Adult ADHD, receives an email from her manager asking her to meet her this week.

She thinks, 'Oh, no! She's going to ask me how the report is going, and I haven't even started it.'

What reactions are likely to follow?

Emotions: ....

Physical sensations: ....

Behaviour: ....

Now, imagine she gets the same email but this time she thinks, 'We have a new trainee starting and she wants us to prepare for that.'

Emotions: ....

Physical sensations: ....

Behaviour: ....

What do you notice? The situation is almost the same; the only thing that has changed is her interpretation of the situation.

Can you think of a recent situation where you noticed your mood change?

What thoughts, emotions, physical feelings and behaviours were involved? You can use Image A5 to record these.

Situation

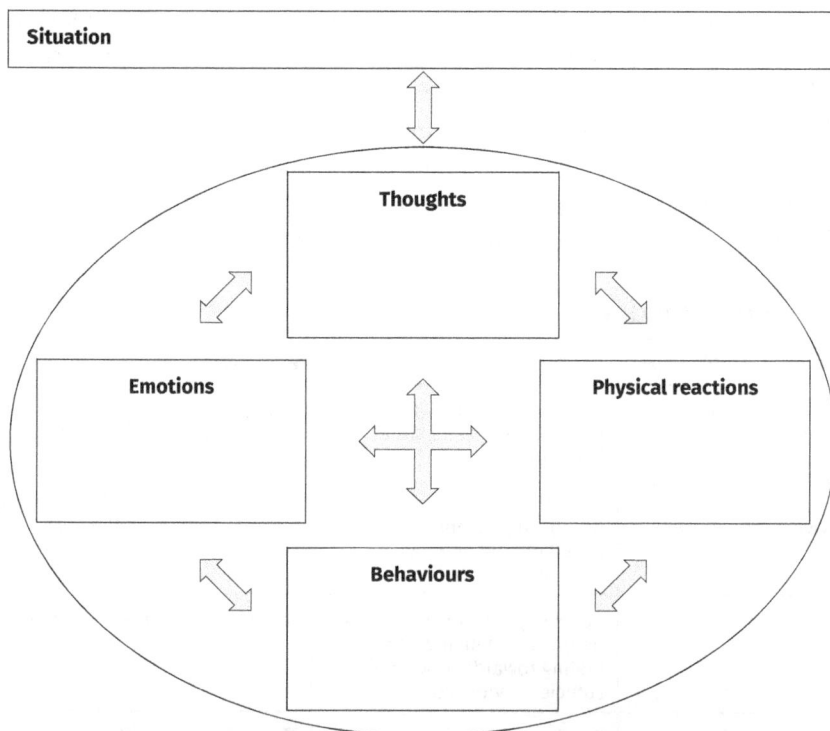

Image A5: CBT five areas: my own recent example

Automatic thoughts

Automatic thoughts come into your mind from moment to moment. With practice, they become easier to spot. Can you notice any thoughts right now? There may be thoughts about this handout or your concentration levels; there may be memories or images.

We tend to believe our thoughts without question. However, they are only an interpretation of events. This means that different people can perceive the same events quite differently. Remember Yemi's email from her manager? As we saw, the same email could lead to more than one interpretation, and from that, different emotions, physical reactions and behaviours. This is affected by previous experience: for example, someone who has been criticized at work would be more likely to anticipate it happening again.

We do not have time to interpret every situation in detail so we rely on generalizations to help us make quick judgements and decisions. One sort of generalization is a stereotype – a commonly held perception that is exaggerated or oversimplified, for example 'All British people love football.'

These help us to make quick judgements and process information quickly, but we may miss useful information that could help us form a fuller or more balanced picture. We give up accuracy for speed. Human thinking is therefore *biased*. An example of a biased thought is someone who gets a question wrong in a quiz and thinks, 'I *never* get anything right.' Some more examples of common thinking biases are included in the table below. Which ones do you notice in your own thinking?

Common thinking biases

Type of thinking bias	Description	Example
All-or-nothing thinking	Categorizing ourselves, people, events and situations in extremes	*Because I didn't get this task right, I am a complete failure; everyone else can do things better than me*
Overgeneralization	Broad-ranging appraisals based on one or a few examples	*I always mess everything up*
Mind-reading	Believing that we know what people are thinking and feeling towards us without sufficient evidence	*My manager thinks I'm stupid*
Catastrophizing/ fortune-telling	Predicting outcomes in a negative way without considering other possible outcomes	*If I don't get to work on time, I will lose my job; I will never manage to do this*
'Should' and 'must' statements	Holding fixed beliefs about the world and how we should act and be treated	*I should always be able to express my thoughts and views clearly*
Negative filtering	Homing in on the negative aspects of a situation whilst ignoring or dismissing positive aspects	*Although I passed my exams, because I did less well than my classmate (who was top of the class), I performed badly*
Emotional reasoning	Using our emotions as evidence for our thoughts or beliefs	*Because I feel anxious/ uncertain, it must mean that I'm doing a bad job*
Jumping to conclusions	Deciding something before having all the facts	*This must be my fault*
Discounting positives	Claiming that positive events are trivial or do not count	*I did well on that project because it was easy*
Personalizing	Placing undue responsibility/ blame on oneself	*My flatmate is in a bad mood because I have done something wrong*

Common thinking patterns in ADHD

We have noted that adults with ADHD tend to report common thinking patterns. They are:

Lack of confidence in their ability to achieve tasks or goals, self-control and reliability. Growing up with ADHD, people may have received negative feedback from those around them. Even if they have not received overt feedback, they may have felt different to, or negatively compared themselves with, classmates or siblings without the same challenges. These experiences can result in unhelpful or biased thoughts about their abilities.

High personal standards. Some people with ADHD make high demands of themselves. They may criticize themselves excessively for mistakes or for things that they have not done. They may also set unrealistic goals, leading to further self-criticism when those goals are not met.

As we have seen, the ways in which we think, including these common thinking patterns, relate to how we behave and how we feel. This also means that by changing how we think about things, we can change the ways we behave and feel.

The first step is to notice automatic thoughts. This will help you identify common thoughts or themes (patterns), the situations where they occur and how they affect your daily life (i.e. the feelings and behaviours that follow).

Have you noticed any common thoughts or patterns in your thinking?

You can find out more by using the Thought Record. Complete this as soon as possible after you notice a change in how you are feeling. In the first shaded section, record thoughts and other experiences as they arise. The 'hot' thought is the one linked to the strongest emotion. If you choose, with support from your therapist, you can then use the unshaded section to challenge hot thoughts and identify helpful alternatives.

Yemi's completed Thought Record

Situation	Thought	Emotion	Physical	Behaviour	Consequence?
	What went through your mind? Rate belief in 'hot' thought (0–100%) Can you spot any thinking biases?	What emotions were around? Rate emotion (0–100%)	What did you feel in your body? Rate intensity (0–100%)	What did you do/ what do you want to do?	What happened?
Took three times longer than my husband to get ready this morning	I haven't got anything done (all or nothing, discounting the positives) I am going to let him down 80% (catastrophizing, fortune-telling)	Irritable 70% Flat 60% Sad 60%	Heavy 70%	Withdraw Hide my feelings Tell myself off	I spent the morning dwelling on it Felt worse, more distractible than usual

↓

Re-frame

	Thought	Emotion	Physical	Behaviour	
	Alternative thought	What emotions are around now? Re-rate emotion (0–100%)	What can you feel in your body now? Rate intensity (0–100%)	What can you do now?	
	I have got some things done We are different, we contribute in different ways Telling myself off just makes me feel worse and makes it harder – I am trying the best I can Belief in hot thought 50%	Irritable 40% Flat 25% Sad 40%	A bit lighter Heavy 45%	Plan for tomorrow morning this evening so I know what I need to do	

Thought Record

Complete this as soon as possible after you notice a change in how you are feeling.

Situation	Thought	Emotion	Physical	Behaviour	Consequence?
	What went through your mind? Rate belief in 'hot' thought (0–100%) Can you spot any thinking biases?	What emotions were around? Rate emotion (0–100%)	What did you feel in your body? Rate intensity (0–100%)	What did you do/ what do you want to do?	What happened?

→

Re-frame

Thought	Emotion	Physical	Behaviour
Alternative thought	What emotions are around now? Re-rate emotion (0–100%)	What can you feel in your body now? Rate intensity (0–100%)	What can you do now?

Questions to ask when evaluating and re-framing the hot thought

1. Is this a thought or a fact?
    - What evidence is there for the thought?
    - Is there any evidence against the thought?
    - Can you spot any thinking biases?

2. What would you say to a friend of yours if they thought the same?

3. Is it possible you are only seeing one part of the situation and ignoring other factors (such as your strengths or positives in the situation)?

4. Are you blaming yourself for something that you cannot control?

5. What are the advantages of thinking this way?

6. ...and what are the disadvantages of thinking this way?

7. What do you feel in your body and what do you want to do when you have this thought?

8. Does this thought move you towards or away from your goal (of...)? Is there another way of thinking about this that would move you towards your goal (i.e. make your desired behaviour more likely to happen)?

Handout summary

- How we think about a situation affects what we do and how we feel.
- Thoughts can be unhelpful or 'biased'.
- By changing how we think, we can change what we do and how we feel.

CORE HANDOUT: MANAGING EMOTIONS AND IMPULSES

Some people say difficulties with emotions are central to their ADHD, for instance their moods are 'up and down' or they have problems with anger. In this handout, we explore how managing emotional experiences can help with this and with other ADHD challenges such as impulsivity and procrastination.

Facts about emotions

Emotions are a natural part of life. While some may feel uncomfortable or distressing, such as fear and sadness, there are also many pleasant emotions such as love and happiness. Our emotions are messages that can help in the following ways:

Looking after our bodies. Emotions such as fear can warn us that we might need to take action for our physical safety.

Looking after ourselves in social situations.

- **Communicating our needs to others**. If we look upset, someone else may see and know we need help.
- **Setting limits**. If we feel uncomfortable or angry with others' behaviour, we can do something about it.

Making decisions. We only know what we want if we know how we feel about the options.

Making lifestyle changes. If we know we feel unhappy with our situation, we can change it.

Although emotions may not always feel good, it is important to remember that they are not harmful. They only become problematic if you judge them as wrong, bad, dangerous or inappropriate and respond to them in unhelpful ways.

Many people have negative beliefs about emotions. For example, they believe that feeling an intense emotion will make them 'go mad' or lose control, that it will go on forever or that they will not be able to stand it. They may believe that just having strong emotions means something bad about them as a person, such as that they are weak or mentally unstable.

In fact, all emotions come and go, however intense they may feel at the time. But, if people have negative beliefs about emotions, they are likely to try to avoid, ignore or suppress them ('bottle them up'). Other ways of managing emotions include drinking alcohol, comfort eating, repeatedly checking social media, gaming and spending money.

While they may provide some relief in the short term, these behaviours may ultimately make you feel far worse, keeping uncomfortable or distressing emotions around for even longer. They place the body under stress and are tiring; they can also lead to physical health problems and mental health problems such as anxiety. Bottled up emotions can come out in unpredictable emotional outbursts, which cause more distress to you and those around you. Most importantly, you will miss the messages that your emotions carry and will not be able to take steps to improve the situation.

Increasing emotional awareness

It can be helpful to identify the situations that trigger strong emotions and to observe the emotions as they arise. Rather than seeing them as 'good' or 'bad', try to look at them with curiosity and interest. Notice what physical reactions in your body accompany these emotions. Ask yourself, 'What was going through my mind just before I started to feel this way?', 'Is this a message that I need to take some action to address the situation?' and 'Even though this feels unpleasant, can I bear it? Does it die down over time?'

For some people, it can be distressing to notice emotions that they may have been avoiding or suppressing, particularly at first. This is especially true for people who have experienced very difficult events in their past. If this is the case, you can discuss this with your therapist, and they will be able to offer further guidance. When working with distressing emotions, it is important that you go at your own pace.

Ways of managing emotions

The list below contains suggested ways of managing emotions. Some are things you may do immediately when you are experiencing intense emotions. Others are things you may do when anticipating a situation that triggers intense emotions. Still others are things you may practise even when feeling calm to help manage intense emotions when they arise.

1. **Calming the body and mind**.
    - Deep breathing.
    - Relaxation.
    - Physical exercise.
    - Pay attention to all the senses – ask yourself 'What can I feel, see, hear?' etc.
    - Identifying and challenging NATs.

2. **Expressing emotions**.
    - Directly expressing to others in the situation how you are feeling.
    - Writing them down in a journal or using an Emotion Diary.
    - Talking to someone you feel close to afterwards.
    - Artistic activities such as music, painting, dance, etc.

3. **Developing greater acceptance of your experience through techniques such as mindfulness**. This helps you to stay with difficult emotions, name them and observe how they come and go, 'allowing' them to be there without acting on them and seeing them as a normal part of life and not as a sign that there is something wrong with you.

Emotion Diary

Date and situation	What is the name of the emotion(s) or feeling(s)? Rate intensity (0–100%)	What can you feel in your body?	Are there any thoughts going through your mind about this emotion?	What does this emotion make you want to do? (What is the impulse?)	What happens if you stop and stay with this experience? Make a note of any observations Re-rate emotional intensity

Emotional experiences and behaviour

Can you think of a recent time when your actions felt 'out of control'? This could have been when you behaved in a way that you or others did not like or that had negative results for you. Examples might be spending too much money impulsively or having an emotional outburst where you expressed your feelings in a way that you would have preferred not to.

Rather than being out of control, another form of behaviour that may relate to difficult emotions could have been not doing something that you needed to do, i.e. putting off or procrastinating.

Here is an example from Ali who found it difficult to stop spending money. Ali found that, despite not having a lot of spare money, he would buy things impulsively. He justified it at the time, telling himself he deserved it or that he was buying gifts for other people rather than himself, but later regretted it and wished he could resist the impulse to spend. The diagram below shows his thoughts, emotions, physical sensations and responses when he makes an impulse purchase.

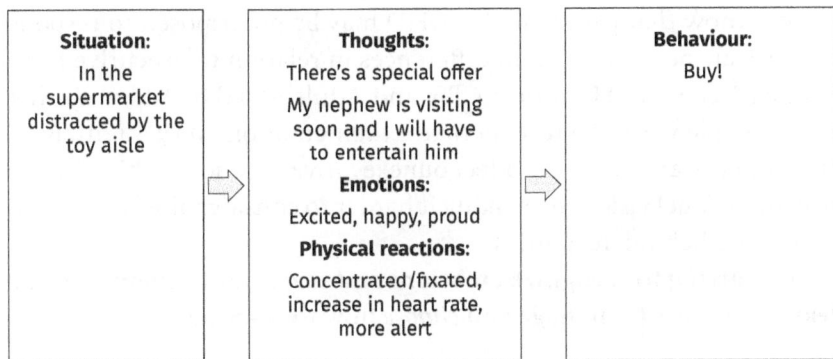

Situation:		Thoughts:		Behaviour:
In the supermarket distracted by the toy aisle	⇨	There's a special offer My nephew is visiting soon and I will have to entertain him **Emotions:** Excited, happy, proud **Physical reactions:** Concentrated/fixated, increase in heart rate, more alert	⇨	Buy!

You will see that Ali's thoughts, emotions and physical reactions lead to behaviours or actions. At the time, these follow on so quickly that they seem automatic; often, it is only when he looks back that he sees all the parts of this process.

Can you think of a recent situation where something similar happened to you? You can use the blank diagram below to write this down.

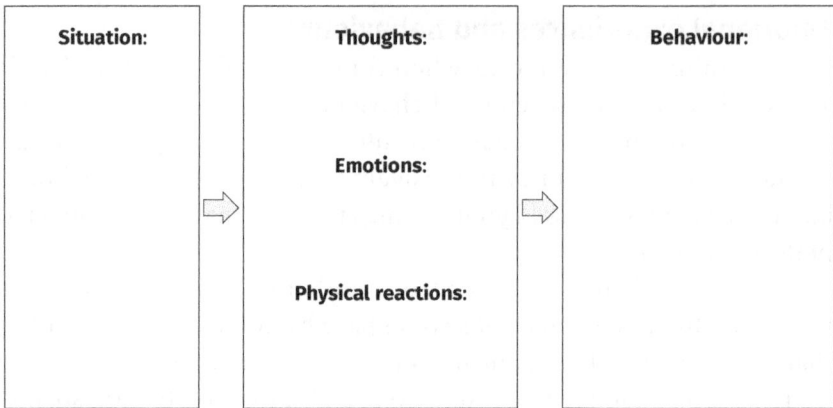

Situation:		Thoughts: Emotions: Physical reactions:		Behaviour:

Impulses

Impulsivity is, of course, a core symptom of ADHD. If you are impulsive, you are likely to act without thinking enough first. Many people with ADHD describe impulses as almost impossible to resist and feel they have little control over their behaviour. Here we use the term 'impulse' to describe an immediate desire to act or respond *to an emotional experience*.

We know that people with ADHD may be predisposed to respond impulsively because of brain differences in relation to executive functioning (see **Core Handout**: CBT and Adult ADHD). Added to this, many people with ADHD experience their emotions very intensely. In turn, intense emotions can affect our executive functions. Thinking can become 'tunnel visioned', making it harder to consider alternative, perhaps more helpful, responses.

In starting to recognize emotions and reactions to them, you can learn new ways to manage and *choose* how to respond.

Responding to impulses

The advantage of impulses is that they help us act on our emotions quickly. We have them because they helped our ancestors to survive, and our ancestors passed on their genes to us. The impulses that often follow fear or anxiety are to run away or to avoid something. Similarly, the impulses that often follow anger are to fight or stand up for something important. (Together, these responses are known as the 'fight or flight' response.) Fear may also lead to the 'freeze' response, i.e. to become immobile or paralyzed in response to a threat you cannot fight or escape from. While we may think of these emotions and impulses as undesirable, they have evolved to protect us – in the case of anger, to defend ourselves, and in the case of fear, to keep us safe from danger.

However, depending on the situation and how we have interpreted it, our first impulses are not necessarily helpful. For example, we may feel fearful about having to talk about our work in front of people and want to avoid it, but it needs to be done as part of the job and probably will not be as bad as we expect.

Emotions, impulses and alternative responses

Emotion	Examples of impulse	Alternative behaviour
Fear or anxiety	Run or get away Avoid, procrastinate	Approach it or engage with it; stay with it
Anger	Fight or 'bottle up' (suppress)	Withdraw if it is risky to fight Communicate one's views and feelings calmly and assertively
Boredom, lack of interest in what one 'should' be doing	Avoid, procrastinate	Stay with task anyway, for example reminding oneself of why it is important to do it and planning more rewarding behaviour after it's finished
Guilt	Get rid of the feeling by distracting oneself with a pleasurable behaviour Try to conceal one's behaviour Apologize excessively to try to prevent others' anger or disapproval	Apologize or take action to make the situation better Apologize only if it is appropriate and to an appropriate amount, taking into account our own needs and rights
Shame	Distract from thinking about oneself, for example with drugs or sex Punish oneself, for example self-criticism, self-harm Hide	Take a self-compassionate view, remind oneself of one's good qualities and that we all make mistakes, and consider if anything needs to be done to address the situation Continue to interact with others, knowing that we all have things we are ashamed of
Interest	Engage immediately to the exclusion of other things	Ignore or let go, return to the current task

The table shows some common emotions, impulses and alternative (and often more helpful) ways of reacting to them. Note that all responses have their place, and it is the *context* that determines which response will be most appropriate or helpful. Most of them are emotions that are often uncomfortable or unpleasant. However, another impulse that is common in relation to ADHD is the urge to immediately follow an interest. Interest can be thought of as an emotion, just as the others in the table, but is usually an enjoyable emotion. Again, though, there are different ways to respond to interest – the impulsive response or an alternative. Similarly, both have their advantages, and it is the context that will determine which response will be most helpful.

Do you struggle with any impulses in particular? What are they?

. . . .

. . . .

What do you do or not do as a result?

. . . .

. . . .

What are the situations or triggers? Do you notice any associated emotions?

. . . .

. . . .

What impact is responding impulsively having on your life (on you and those around you)?

. . . .

. . . .

Are you aware of any alternative responses that may be more helpful?

. . . .

. . . .

What makes impulse challenges worse?

Impulses may become problematic if we respond to them all the time or out of desperation when emotions feel intolerable. It is a fact of life that we will face situations that make us bored, nervous, upset, angry or frustrated. If we are in the habit of always following the impulse, we never learn how to manage these emotions in other, more helpful, ways.

Impulsive responses are maintained because, in the short term at least, they make us feel good in some way. This is either because something pleasant happens – for example the rush of pleasure when buying something ('a dopamine hit') – or something that feels bad goes away or reduces – for example the feelings of uncertainty or discomfort around a task when procrastinating.

No wonder then that so many people follow impulses when they arise. While this feels good in the short term, in the longer term it usually feels worse – this is because an initial situation has not been dealt with or the impulsive response has caused an additional problem, such as debt from impulsive spending.

Image A7 shows what happens when Ali follows his impulse to buy things. When he sees a toy that he knows his nephew would like, he feels excited, happy and proud, and this leads him to follow the impulse and buy the toy. Immediately (short-term consequence), he feels a rush of excitement and pleasure as he imagines how happy his nephew will be. Later, though (long-term consequence), he thinks about having spent money he could not afford and about his ability to resist the impulse to buy things, and he feels regret, remorse and sadness. His self-criticism and view of this impulsive action as reflecting a permanent characteristic of himself undermine his confidence in his ability to resist temptation and make it harder to resist the impulse next time.

Similarly, when we feel anxious about completing a piece of work, we may have the impulse or urge to avoid it or procrastinate. While avoiding the task makes us feel better in the short term, in the longer term, we feel more anxious since the task is not done. Also, we do not learn skills to help us complete the task, we do not have the chance to find out we can do it and we feel less confident, so we are more likely to avoid it in the future.

Acting on angry feelings while still in the full intensity of the feeling can lead to fights or arguments. In the short term, it may feel good to release angry feelings and make ourselves heard, and sometimes it is appropriate (e.g. to protect someone who is in danger), but at other times it can lead to destructive consequences. It also prevents us from learning more effective solutions and ways to manage angry feelings. In the longer term, there may be more painful emotions such as guilt, regret or sadness.

Interest spurs us to engage with something, to explore and find out more, and as such it helps us grow, develop and discover. However, following interest becomes a problem if we do this at the expense of tasks that are more monotonous or routine but necessary. Whilst life may be spontaneous and exciting, always following the impulse to switch from boring to more interesting tasks may mean you do not develop effective habits to manage monotonous or routine tasks. This can lead to backlogs, overwhelm and frustration.

Becoming aware of impulsive responses and their consequences can help us to slow them down, allowing the chance to make different decisions. An important part of this is understanding more about emotions and ways of managing them.

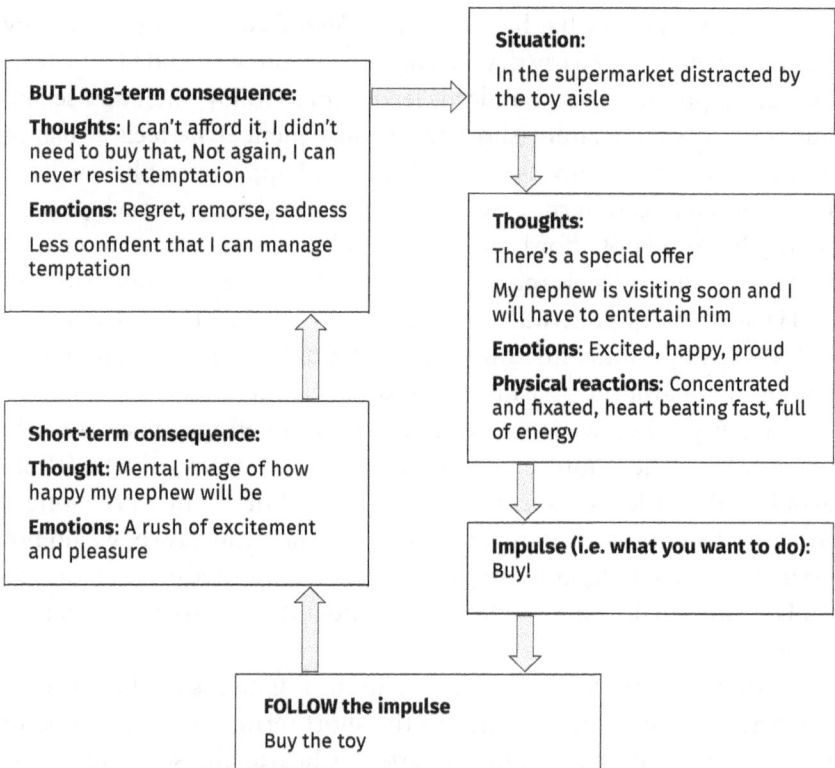

Situation:
In the supermarket distracted by the toy aisle

BUT Long-term consequence:
Thoughts: I can't afford it, I didn't need to buy that, Not again, I can never resist temptation
Emotions: Regret, remorse, sadness
Less confident that I can manage temptation

Thoughts:
There's a special offer
My nephew is visiting soon and I will have to entertain him
Emotions: Excited, happy, proud
Physical reactions: Concentrated and fixated, heart beating fast, full of energy

Short-term consequence:
Thought: Mental image of how happy my nephew will be
Emotions: A rush of excitement and pleasure

Impulse (i.e. what you want to do): Buy!

FOLLOW the impulse
Buy the toy

Image A7: Following the impulse

Resisting impulses using the Stop! Stay! Choose! strategy

This strategy enables you to notice the emotional experience (including the thoughts, physical reactions and emotions) driving the impulse and manage it differently. First, try to delay responding (Stop!). This allows time to consider both the short-term and the longer-term consequences of decisions (Stay!). This 'bigger picture' view helps you resist the most immediate (and tempting) response and to take (Choose!) actions that may be more helpful in the longer term, including ways of coping with strong emotions.

When you feel an impulse to do something:

Stop!

Pause, take a breath.

Identify your experience at this moment:

. . . .

. . . .

What is going through your mind? (thoughts, images)

. . . .

. . . .

What are you feeling in your body? (physical sensations)

. . . .

. . . .

Can you name your emotion(s)?

. . . .

. . . .

What is the impulse or action urge – what do you want to do right now?

. . . .

. . . .

Ali noticed that he was feeling excited, happy and proud, he was concentrated and fixated on the toy he wanted to buy, his heart was beating fast, he felt full of energy and he was thinking about his nephew and imagining how happy he would be. He had a strong impulse to buy his nephew the toy.

Stay!

Can you allow and accept these thoughts, physical sensations, emotions? Try and stay with them even if it is difficult. Try not to either push them away or make them stronger.

Try to resist the impulse (the immediate urge to act or avoid).
    What do you notice?

. . . .

. . . .

Ali said that as he stayed with the thoughts, emotions and physical sensations, they remained strong at first; however, he was able to observe them with curiosity and prevent himself from following the impulse. This allowed him time to think things through. He was able to think to himself, 'Does he need it? I have already got him some presents and overspending has got me in trouble before.'

Choose!

Choose your response. What can you do now instead of following the impulse? (E.g. pick a small part of a project and work on it for just ten minutes, plan what you will say to your friend when you feel a bit calmer or talk to someone for support.)

. . . .

. . . .

Ali took some deep breaths to calm himself and physically turned away from the toy, looking at his shopping list and walking towards the things he had planned to buy. At first, he felt disappointed and restless but he noticed that the emotion and physical feelings subsided quite quickly as he focused his attention elsewhere.

Image A8 illustrates the Stop! Stay! Choose! strategy.

STOP!	STAY!	CHOOSE!
Pause, take a breath Notice: Thoughts and images Physical sensations Emotion(s) – rate how strong (0–100%) Impulse	Can you allow and accept these thoughts, physical sensations, emotions? Try to stay with them even if it is difficult Try not to either push them away or make them stronger Try to resist the impulse (the immediate urge to act or avoid) What do you notice? Re-rate the emotions	Choose your response What can you do now instead of following the impulse? (alternative behaviour) For example, pick a small part of a task and work on it for just ten minutes, plan what to say to your friend when you're feeling a bit calmer What can you do now to manage your emotions?

Image A8: Stop! Stay! Choose!

The following questions may help when choosing how to respond:

- What will happen if I follow the impulse?
  - What would happen in the short term?
  - But what would the long-term consequences be?

- What will happen if I stop and stay?
  - How will I feel in the short term?
  - Even though this may be uncomfortable, would I be able to stand this?
  - What will be the long-term benefits?

- What can I do now?
  - What is the alternative behaviour to the impulse?
  - What can I do to manage any uncomfortable emotions? For example, breathing exercises, self-soothing.

Image A9 shows how Ali resisted the impulse by using Stop! Stay! Choose!

You can use Image A10 to identify what happens when you follow the impulse and when you resist it. You can also use the Impulse Log to record events as they occur.

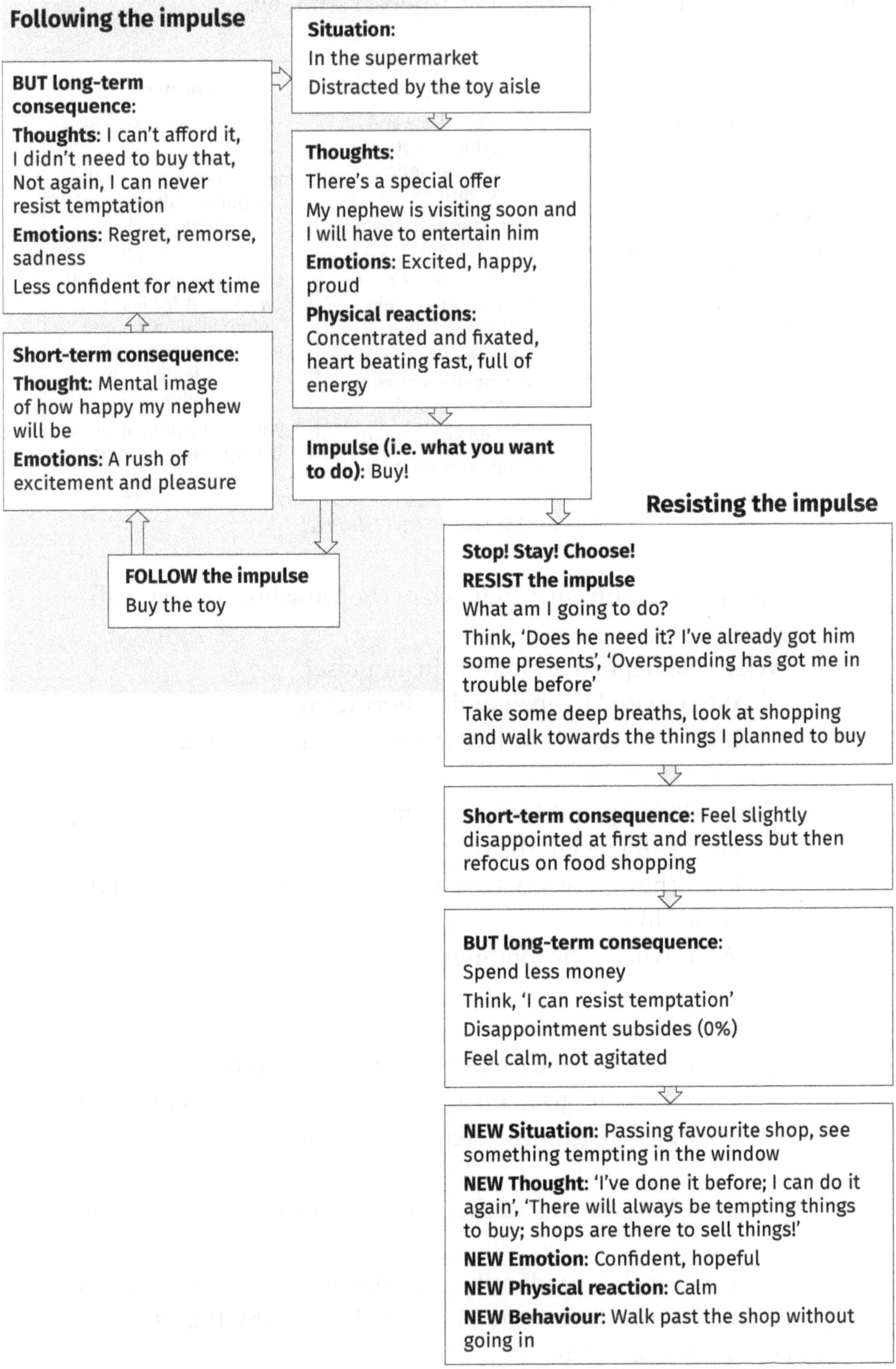

Following the impulse

Situation:
In the supermarket
Distracted by the toy aisle

Thoughts:
There's a special offer
My nephew is visiting soon and I will have to entertain him
Emotions: Excited, happy, proud
Physical reactions: Concentrated and fixated, heart beating fast, full of energy

Impulse (i.e. what you want to do): Buy!

BUT long-term consequence:
Thoughts: I can't afford it, I didn't need to buy that, Not again, I can never resist temptation
Emotions: Regret, remorse, sadness
Less confident for next time

Short-term consequence:
Thought: Mental image of how happy my nephew will be
Emotions: A rush of excitement and pleasure

FOLLOW the impulse
Buy the toy

Resisting the impulse

Stop! Stay! Choose!
RESIST the impulse
What am I going to do?
Think, 'Does he need it? I've already got him some presents', 'Overspending has got me in trouble before'
Take some deep breaths, look at shopping and walk towards the things I planned to buy

Short-term consequence: Feel slightly disappointed at first and restless but then refocus on food shopping

BUT long-term consequence:
Spend less money
Think, 'I can resist temptation'
Disappointment subsides (0%)
Feel calm, not agitated

NEW Situation: Passing favourite shop, see something tempting in the window
NEW Thought: 'I've done it before; I can do it again', 'There will always be tempting things to buy; shops are there to sell things!'
NEW Emotion: Confident, hopeful
NEW Physical reaction: Calm
NEW Behaviour: Walk past the shop without going in

Image A9: Resisting the impulse using Stop! Stay! Choose!

Following the impulse

BUT long-term consequence:

Situation:

Thoughts:

Emotions:

Physical reactions:

Short-term consequence:

Impulse (i.e. what you want to do):

FOLLOW the impulse

Resisting the impulse

Stop! Stay! Choose!
RESIST the impulse
What am I going to do?

Short-term consequence:

BUT long-term consequence:

NEW Situation:

NEW Thought:

NEW Emotion:

NEW Physical reaction:

NEW Behaviour:

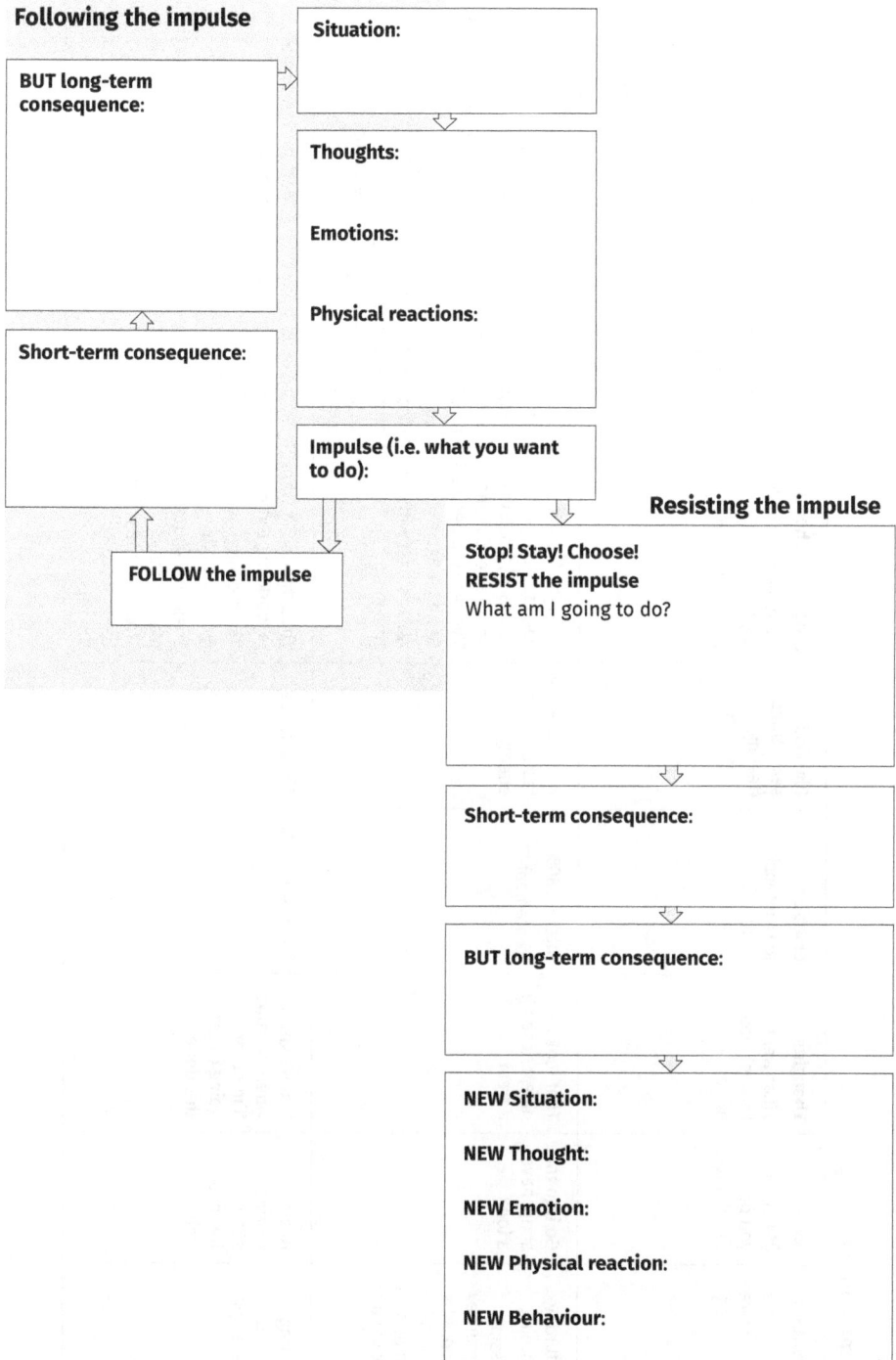

Image A10: Blank Following and Resisting the impulse diagram to complete

Example Impulse Log

Situation Date, time, what were you doing?	Impulse (What did you feel like doing?)	Thoughts What went through your mind?	Emotions Rate intensity (0-100%)	Physical sensations (feelings in your body)	Stop! Stay! Choose! What did you think or say to yourself? What did you do?	What happened at first? What thoughts, emotions (rate 0-100%), physical sensations were there at first? (Short-term consequence)	Outcome What happened next? What thoughts, emotions (rate 0-100%), physical sensations followed? (Long-term consequence)
Saturday morning Passing favourite shop, saw something tempting in the window	Go into the shop, have a look	That looks nice, I deserve a treat	Interest 80% Excitement 75%	Heart beating faster, full of energy	Thought, 'I don't need to buy anything', 'I'm trying not to spend money', 'I've resisted before, I can do it again' Walked past without going in	Continued to think about going into the shop: 'what if I missed out on something nice?' Felt slightly disappointed (30%) and restless but carried on walking away	Spent less money Thought, 'I can resist temptation' Soon forgot about the shop Disappointment subsided (0%) Felt calm
Writing report, Weds 3pm	Avoid writing, search for music online	'I don't know where to start', 'I'm never going to get this done'	Frustrated 80%	Tired, tense	Thought 'I don't want to work late today' 'Good enough is good enough' Spent 15 minutes planning the structure and writing the first paragraph of the report	Felt anxious at first (50%) but this did not last as long as I thought it would	Made progress on report anxious 5%, proud 75% Increased energy Thought: 'I can do this'

Impulse Log

Situation Date, time, what were you doing?	Impulse (What did you feel like doing?)	Thoughts What went through your mind?	Emotions Rate intensity (0-100%)	Physical sensations (feelings in your body)	Stop! Stay! Choose! What did you think or say to yourself? What did you do?	What happened at first? What thoughts, emotions (rate 0-100%), physical sensations were there at first? (Short-term consequence)	Outcome What happened next? What thoughts, emotions (rate 0-100%), physical sensations followed? (Long-term consequence)

Handout summary

- Emotions are a natural part of life, and even though they do not always feel good, they carry important messages.
- Unhelpful ways of managing emotions can worsen problems with impulsivity or procrastination.
- In starting to recognize emotions and reactions to them, you can learn new ways to manage and choose how to respond.

SUPPLEMENTARY HANDOUT: PROCRASTINATION

Procrastination is another word for putting things off. This usually means doing less important or more interesting tasks instead of more urgent, important, difficult or boring ones. Some people call this 'task paralysis'.

Everyone procrastinates sometimes; however, it becomes a problem when it is a habitual response to demands or deadlines. Challenges such as impulsivity and distractibility make procrastination more likely, so it is perhaps unsurprising that many adults with ADHD procrastinate.

Procrastination is likely to occur when a task:

- is associated with an uncomfortable emotion such as anxiety, dread or boredom
- seems overwhelming or unmanageable – perhaps there are thoughts that it will take too long or will be too difficult.

Often there is uncertainty, perhaps in predicting how long something will take, knowing what to do or doubting your abilities.

Common thoughts that keep procrastination going
Thoughts about the task itself

- It will take ages.
- It will be really difficult.
- It's too boring.
- I don't know how to do it.

Self-criticism

- I should have done this before.

Anticipation of 'failure' or criticism

- I won't do it well enough.
- I need to do it perfectly (perfectionism).
- Even if I try, I won't be able to do it.

Permission-giving thoughts (that excuse procrastination)

- I shouldn't have to do this.

- I can do it later.
- I need the pressure of a deadline to get the motivation.
- I work best late at night.
- I have to be in the right mood to get started.

Procrastination cycle

The procrastination cycle is shown in Image A11. When the task is avoided, there is often an immediate sense of relief from the uncomfortable thoughts, physical sensations and emotions. If something more pleasurable is done instead, there may also be enjoyment. Since the immediate short-term consequence is pleasant, avoidance is rewarded. Behaviour that is rewarded becomes more frequent and so the cycle of avoidance continues.

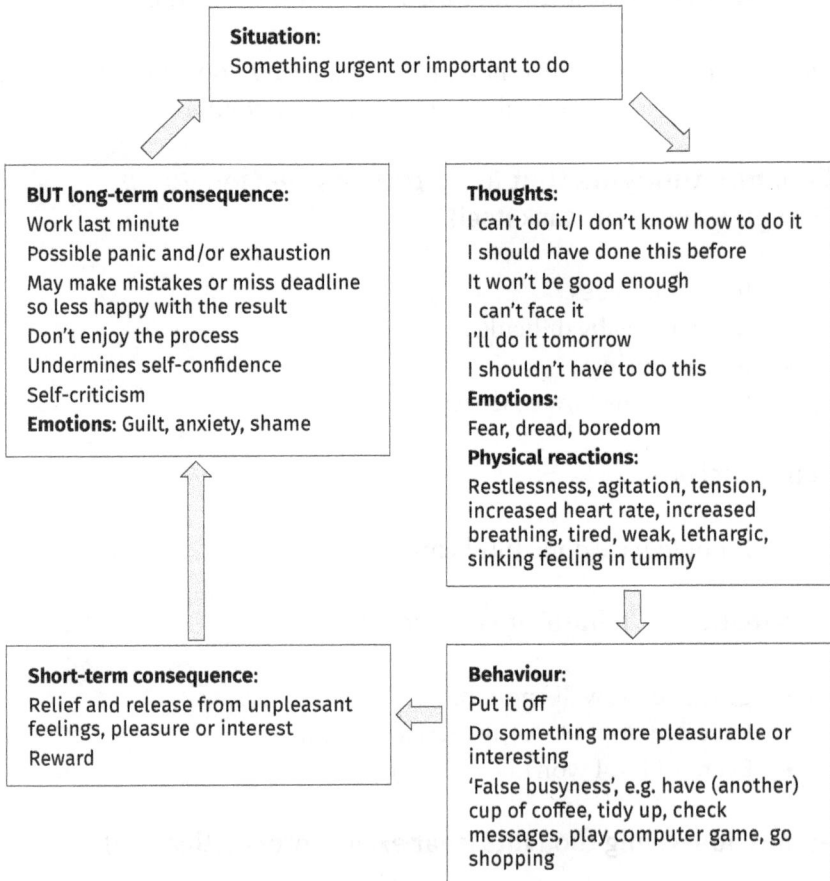

Situation:
Something urgent or important to do

BUT long-term consequence:
Work last minute
Possible panic and/or exhaustion
May make mistakes or miss deadline so less happy with the result
Don't enjoy the process
Undermines self-confidence
Self-criticism
Emotions: Guilt, anxiety, shame

Thoughts:
I can't do it/I don't know how to do it
I should have done this before
It won't be good enough
I can't face it
I'll do it tomorrow
I shouldn't have to do this
Emotions:
Fear, dread, boredom
Physical reactions:
Restlessness, agitation, tension, increased heart rate, increased breathing, tired, weak, lethargic, sinking feeling in tummy

Short-term consequence:
Relief and release from unpleasant feelings, pleasure or interest
Reward

Behaviour:
Put it off
Do something more pleasurable or interesting
'False busyness', e.g. have (another) cup of coffee, tidy up, check messages, play computer game, go shopping

Image A11: The procrastination cycle

Unfortunately, because the task has not been completed, the uncomfortable emotions, such as anxiety, increase and there may also be some new feelings, such as guilt – this is the long-term consequence. Confidence in the ability to do it, and to tolerate the difficult initial feelings, will have decreased and so it will seem more overwhelming or unmanageable next time. The combination of the short-term consequence and the long-term consequence make avoidance more likely the next time, and so the cycle repeats.

Sometimes the task is put off indefinitely. Alternatively, it gets done but at the last minute. In this case, the cycle is still repeated: the initial avoidance is still reinforced and the later process of completing the task at the last minute is likely to be stressful, exhausting or unsatisfying, bringing more uncomfortable emotions.

Overall, procrastination leads to self-critical thinking (e.g. about wasted time or missed opportunities) and feeling stressed or low in mood, and it undermines confidence in getting things done maintaining negative self-beliefs.

What do you put off?

. . . .

. . . .

. . . .

. . . .

What is the impact of this?

. . . .

. . . .

. . . .

. . . .

You can use the blank procrastination cycle in Image A12 to identify the thoughts, emotions, physical sensations, behaviours and short-term and long-term consequences for your own procrastination.

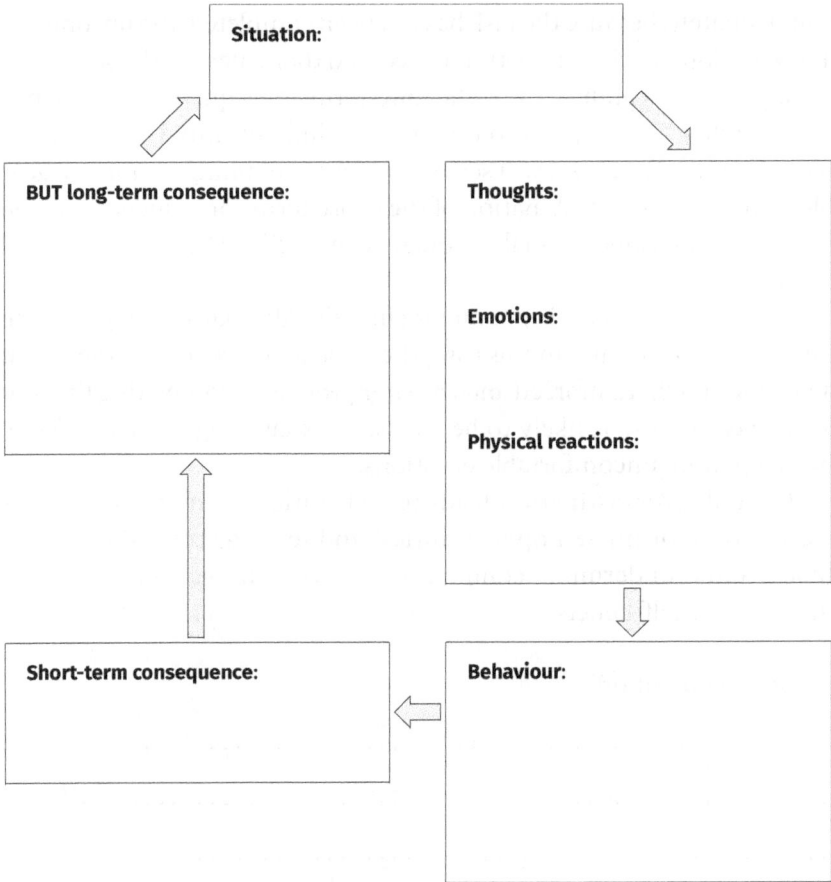

Image A12: My procrastination cycle

Note that this cycle is the same as the Following the impulse cycle in **Core Handout**: Managing Emotions and Impulses.

Managing procrastination

The Stop! Stay! Choose! approach described in **Core Handout**: Managing Emotions and Impulses can be used to manage procrastination. This allows you to notice the experience (including thoughts, physical sensations and emotions), think through different options and choose an alternative, more helpful, response. You may find it helpful to complete the Resisting the impulse diagram in the same handout (see Image A10). It may also help to identify and challenge negative automatic thoughts (NATs) including those related to self-criticism and perfectionism. Here are some other things you can try.

Raise energy levels

Do something that raises your heart rate slightly – move around, run, dance or listen to music.

Approach the task

- Write down what needs to be done, prioritize and schedule when it will be done. Put this in your diary/calendar and set a reminder/timer. Choose a time of day when you feel most energized.
- If it is a written task, start with the main ideas – open a document and write some headings or make a mind map.
- Break big tasks down into smaller 'bite-size' chunks or subtasks – be specific about what you aim to do at each stage.
- Decide how long you will spend on each subtask and use a timer to help you stick to this. At first, it is a good idea to start with very small chunks of time, even as little as two minutes, and then increase them as you feel more confident in being able to stay on task for longer periods.
- Reduce distractions – turn off messages, find somewhere quiet to work.
- Reward yourself for every step achieved, however small; if you notice self-critical thoughts, try to talk kindly to yourself instead.

Take breaks

- Plan breaks at regular intervals.
- Before a break, identify the next part of the task so you know what to do when you return.
- If you are having trouble concentrating after trying the tips above, take your mind off the task and do something else for a few minutes (some exercise, talk to someone, have something to eat or drink), setting a timer to return to the task.
- Make time for enjoyable activities and relaxation every day, not just when you finish a big task or project.

Get support

Ask someone to help plan the task, plan 'check in' meetings with you for you to work towards or to work alongside you (body doubling).

SUPPLEMENTARY HANDOUT: ANGER
Problems with anger

Many people with adult ADHD report difficulties with irritability and anger. Anger is a normal human emotion (see **Core Handout**: Managing Emotions and Impulses for more information) and it has an important role. Anger helps us recognize when something is unjust or wrong and gives us the energy and motivation to do something about it. However, it becomes a problem if we get angry a lot of the time or easily lose our temper. It can affect our daily life and our mental wellbeing and upset and frighten those around us. It can have other very serious consequences such as risking others' safety as well as getting into trouble at work or with the law.

Typical triggers and thoughts

Common triggers to anger are believing that we are being disrespected, deceived, attacked or treated unfairly. We are likely to feel angry when others break our personal 'rules' about how people should behave – the stronger and more rigid the rules, the more likely we are to feel angry. Thoughts may include 'This is unacceptable', 'I can't let them get away with this', 'This isn't fair', 'I can't cope with this right now.' (See **Core Handout**: Thinking Patterns in ADHD and **Core Handout**: Beliefs and Coping for more information about thoughts and underlying beliefs.)

Physical sensations of anger

The combination of reactions to these triggers is known as the 'fight or flight' response, which is a survival mechanism to deal with threat, both real and imagined. When this happens, adrenaline is quickly released into the bloodstream, and it has the following physical effects:

- pounding heart (to get more blood to the muscles)
- increased breathing rate (to carry more oxygen to the muscles, via the blood)
- tension in the muscles (readiness for action)
- clenched fists or jaw
- flushed face and neck
- feeling hot and sweaty
- light-headedness
- shaking
- stomach churning or 'butterflies'.

Unhelpful angry behaviour

When we are angry, the impulse is to fight. People express anger in different ways.

Unhelpful ways to respond to anger include the following:

> **Outward aggression.** Snapping, arguing, storming out of situations, shouting, swearing, hitting, breaking things, being verbally abusive, threatening or violent to others.
>
> **Inward aggression.** Saying unkind things to yourself, not allowing yourself basic needs (such as food) or things that you enjoy, isolating yourself from others or harming yourself.
>
> **Non-violent or passive aggression.** Expressing anger in an indirect way by sulking, ignoring others, being sarcastic, refusing to do things, putting them off or doing them poorly.

Image A13 illustrates an anger cycle.

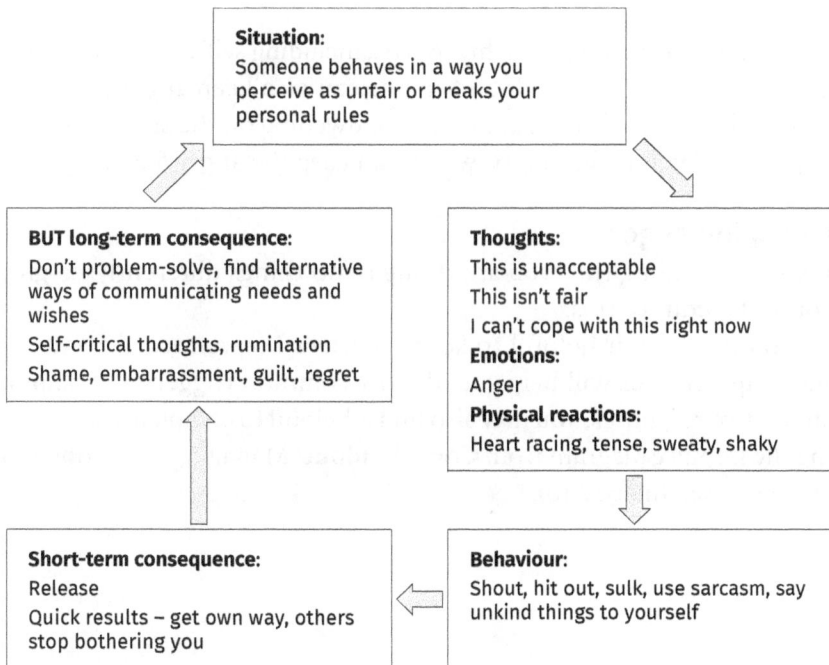

Image A13: Anger cycle

Why might people with ADHD have problems with anger?

ADHD affects emotional regulation, so it can make anger outbursts more likely. Having ADHD challenges can cause frustration, so it may take less to make you feel angry. It is a bit like heating a pan of water – if the water is already hot, it takes less time for it to boil and bubble over than if heating it from cold. In a similar way, if you are already feeling angry (your emotional 'temperature' is rising), it takes less to trigger an outburst than when you are feeling calm. Impulsivity can make it harder to manage strong emotions such as anger once they arise.

What keeps it going?

There are benefits to anger – in the short term at least. It can feel good to release it, can make you feel powerful and can have quick results. For example, if you lose your temper, you may get your own way or stop someone bothering you. This short-term 'reward' makes you more likely to repeat the behaviour. It also prevents you from developing more constructive ways of managing the situation such as problem-solving or communication.

Negative automatic thoughts (NATs), including self-critical thoughts, and emotions such as guilt and shame can also keep anger problems going. There may also be rumination or dwelling on the situations that have caused you to feel angry, which can keep the angry feelings going.

Managing anger

If you are reading this, you are trying to do things differently, so give yourself credit for this.

You may find it helpful to keep an Anger Log to record events as they happen. This will help you identify common triggers and helpful alternative responses. You may also find it helpful to complete the Resisting the impulse diagram from **Core Handout**: Managing Emotions and Impulses (see Image A10).

Anger Log

Trigger What happened? Who was there, what was said and done?	Thoughts What went through your mind? What did the situation mean to you?	Emotion How intense was it? (0–100%)	Physical sensations	Your response What did you say/do?	Short-term consequence	Long-term consequence	Was there an alternative, more helpful response? Is there anything you could have said / done instead?

Our emotions carry important information. Anger can be a sign that we need to do something about a situation to look after ourselves and those around us. The Stop! Stay! Choose! approach described in **Core Handout**: Managing Emotions and Impulses can be used to support this process. In the first instance, this will 'buy' you some time and allow the physical reactions to subside. This makes it easier for you to notice the emotions, think through different options and choose alternative, more helpful responses.

Wise responses to anger
Cool off
If possible, delay responding. This will allow the anger to peak (if it has not already) and then subside. If possible, withdraw from the situation that is making you angry. Leaving the room or going for a walk around the block may help. It usually takes about an hour for the adrenaline levels to go down – if you return to the situation before this, you may find your anger rising once again to a level that is difficult to manage.

Relaxation
Relaxation skills such as breathing exercises, progressive muscle relaxation or imagining relaxing scenes can reduce tension.

Physical activity
Exercise can help release tension and manage physical agitation.

Problem-solving
Your therapist can help you identify the problem and possible solutions.

Communicate assertively
The alternative to responding aggressively is to be assertive, that is to communicate views and feelings calmly, clearly and firmly. Assertiveness means also considering the wishes, views and feelings of others as well as yourself so that each person's or party's rights are respected.

For example:

Your housemate comes in late, slamming the door and waking you up: 'Please close the door quietly when you come in because I am a light sleeper.'

At work you are asked to do something at short notice: 'I would be happy to do that, but could we talk about priorities so that I get the most important things done?'

Someone pushes in front of you in a queue: 'Excuse me, I have been waiting a while – please could you wait your turn?'

Wherever possible, use 'I' statements instead of 'you', as these allow you to communicate your views without sounding accusatory. Think carefully about your non-verbal communication, i.e. your tone of voice (calm) and your body language (e.g. relaxed posture, open uncrossed arms).

Your therapist can help you identify and practise assertive responses. It takes practice to communicate clearly, so do not be discouraged if it feels awkward or does not go smoothly the first time. It will help if you can think about it from the other person's point of view and, if possible, find a solution that works for you both.

Challenge NATs and self-beliefs

Your therapist can help you identify the role of thoughts and beliefs in anger and help you learn ways to manage these.

CORE HANDOUT: BELIEFS AND COPING

In looking at your thoughts more closely, as you have done in previous handouts, you may have started to notice certain patterns of thinking or themes. These patterns or themes point to more general or underlying beliefs.

In **Core Handout**: Thinking Patterns in ADHD we looked at automatic thoughts, which are *situation specific*. In this handout, we will look at more general beliefs that are around much of the time but that may not be so apparent. There are two kinds: core beliefs and rules for living (sometimes called assumptions).

Core beliefs

Core beliefs are deeply held beliefs about ourselves, other people or the world that result from our experiences. If we have had difficult or negative experiences, we may have come to negative conclusions about ourselves. We call this low self-esteem.

Core beliefs, particularly negative ones, are understandable conclusions given our experiences; however, they are inaccurate because they are 'overgeneralizations', even misunderstandings. In many cases, they develop when we are too young to have a broader view of the world and our place within it. Because we presume our core beliefs are true, we tend not to challenge them. What is more, we tend to pay attention to information that confirms them rather than look for information that disproves them (known as the 'confirmatory bias').

Examples are:

Negative	Positive
I am a failure	I am good enough
I am not important	I am valuable and worthwhile
I am unlovable	I am lovable
Other people are more interesting and competent than me	I am as interesting and competent as other people

Note that negative core beliefs are more 'absolute' and inflexible than positive ones.

See the following case example for more information about Yemi, our fictional client. It describes her predispositions, her experiences and how she developed the core belief, 'I am not good enough.'

Case example: Yemi

Predisposition: Yemi said she is very good at details and arguing cases and has a strong sense of logic. She said sometimes this can lead to being 'overfocused', 'obsessive', 'absent-minded' and 'scatty'. Yemi described herself as friendly, warm and expressive. She said she has always been sensitive and feels emotions intensely.

Experiences: Yemi's parents moved to the UK from Nigeria before she was born. She described her childhood as 'comfortable' and 'happy' and her parents as 'supportive'. She thinks her mother 'probably has ADHD', though her father is very organized. Yemi was one of only a few Black girls at her school, and as a result, she said she always felt different: 'Almost no one there looked like me.' At school she was diagnosed with dyslexia. As a result of feeling different and the challenges from her dyslexia (which she now thinks were also part of undiagnosed ADHD), she felt 'not good enough' and that she needed to work 'twice as hard' as the others to be good enough. She put in a lot of effort to do this, and she got positive feedback from family and school for her excellent results. She said, 'It felt really good, and I think I learned to seek external validation.'

When she went to university, she needed to work more than at school, and she struggled with organization and completing her assignments. In the end, she needed to repeat a year. She later trained as a lawyer. By this time, she had learned some coping strategies, but she said she lacked confidence and 'massively overworked' to get through.

In her first jobs, Yemi had problems completing projects on time, and this led to beliefs about being 'unreliable'. Yemi is doing well in her current work and she has been able to shape her role so that she can focus on what she is good at. Yemi thinks though that if her current managers and colleagues knew about her ADHD, they would think badly of her, and it would impact negatively on her job prospects. So, she keeps a check on herself in the office: while moving around and fidgeting help her concentrate, she does not do this as she fears others would disapprove.

Rules for living (assumptions)

To cope with negative core beliefs, we develop 'rules for living'. These are the rules that we must follow to minimize the possibility of the core belief being triggered. For example, Yemi believes herself to be not good enough, but as long as she works very hard at all times, she feels OK about herself.

Just as for core beliefs, we are not explicitly taught our 'rules for

197

living'. We infer them either from our direct experiences or from observing others. Having rules is not in itself a bad thing – realistic and flexible rules, or perhaps *guidelines*, can be healthy and helpful. For example, a helpful rule or guideline would be 'It is good to eat a balanced diet' because there is plenty of evidence to show this is best for us. However, there is also some flexibility in this statement which allows it to be relaxed at certain times, such as celebrations.

Unhelpful rules are usually inflexible. They may include the words 'should' or 'if...then':

- 'I should be able to manage on my own without asking for help.'
- 'I should never make mistakes.'

Or:

- 'If I fail at one task, then I am a complete failure.'

Often, when rules are broken, or are at risk of being broken. there will be a noticeable change in mood. Broken rules tend to lead to low mood; when a rule is not yet broken but there is a risk it might be, this usually results in anxiety.

Yemi identified that she had the following rules for living:

- I need to be brilliant to compensate for being unreliable.
- If people see the real me, I will be rejected.
- I should control my emotions at all times, otherwise I will be rejected.

How unhelpful beliefs lead to unhelpful coping

Such rules are very difficult for someone to follow all the time. While when they started, they were protective and helped you feel OK, in the long run, they end up making you feel worse. This is because they can lead to behaviours that are unsustainable or unhealthy, such as working for long periods without a break, and can prevent healthy behaviours, such as seeking support. Because rules are hard, even impossible, to keep to, we are bound to break them, triggering the core belief and the strong feelings that go with it. Unhelpful rules therefore trap us in unhelpful and ultimately self-defeating patterns of behaviour.

Yemi noticed several compensatory strategies. First, she always worked hard, and she noticed that she expected brilliance – perfection even – from herself in order to feel she was doing well enough. Sometimes the fear of not being able to reach this impossible standard led her to put off her work, i.e. procrastinate.

Yemi also noticed that her belief 'If people see the real me, they will reject me' was leading to hiding her ADHD at work. She knew she would be able to concentrate better if she got up and moved in the day and allowed herself to fidget; however, she was worried that this would be perceived negatively by her colleagues. As a result, she stayed seated during the day. She also had never asked for support and felt unsure about whether it would be helpful to disclose her dyslexia or her ADHD diagnoses at work. She realized that, as a result, she felt resentful when she was expected to work in ways that did not suit her, for example in the middle of an open-plan office.

Yemi said that her fears around others' perceptions of her led to her suppressing other things about herself, including her feelings. A sensitive and expressive person, she had fears of being seen as too emotional ('too much'). She was particularly worried about voicing frustration and irritation, saying she feared being seen as 'an angry Black woman' (a derogatory racial stereotype). As a result, she kept quiet in social situations and at work, and held back from expressing her views, which in turn led to more frustration. When she did occasionally express anger by snapping at her husband, she felt guilty and was highly self-critical.

Yemi realized that these compensatory strategies were contributing to her feeling overwhelmed and exhausted.

Image A14 shows how core beliefs and rules for living develop, using Yemi's examples. It shows how core beliefs and rules for living lead to understandable, but usually unhelpful, coping behaviours.

Predisposition

(e.g. ADHD characteristics, personality, cognitive strengths and differences, energy levels, risk-taking):

Good at details, arguing cases

'Overfocused', absent-minded, scatty

Warm and expressive

Sensitive, feels emotions intensely

Childhood experiences

(e.g. criticism, bullying, abuse, lack of praise from others, loss, neglect, rejection):

Family life comfortable and supportive. Mother – ADHD?

Felt like the odd one out at school – dyslexia and one of only a few Black girls

Believed had to work twice as hard to be just as good

Worked hard – excellent results

Struggled with assignments at university, overworked when training and at work to 'get by', problems completing projects on time

Core belief:

I am not good enough

Rules for living:

I need to be brilliant to compensate for being unreliable

If people see the real me, then I will be rejected

I should control my emotions at all times, otherwise I will be rejected

Compensatory strategies:

Expect perfection from myself and work extra hours to achieve it, 'over-perform', get caught up in the detail

Procrastinate (because I don't think my work will be good enough)

Hide my ADHD — try not to get up too much or fidget at work

Keep quiet – I don't express my feelings or ask for what I want because I'm afraid of being seen as 'too much' or aggressive

Effects of compensatory strategies:

Overwhelm and exhaustion

My ADHD characteristics are worse — harder to concentrate, I feel more restless, I feel frustrated which makes it even harder to manage my emotions

I can't be 'my true self', not meeting my potential

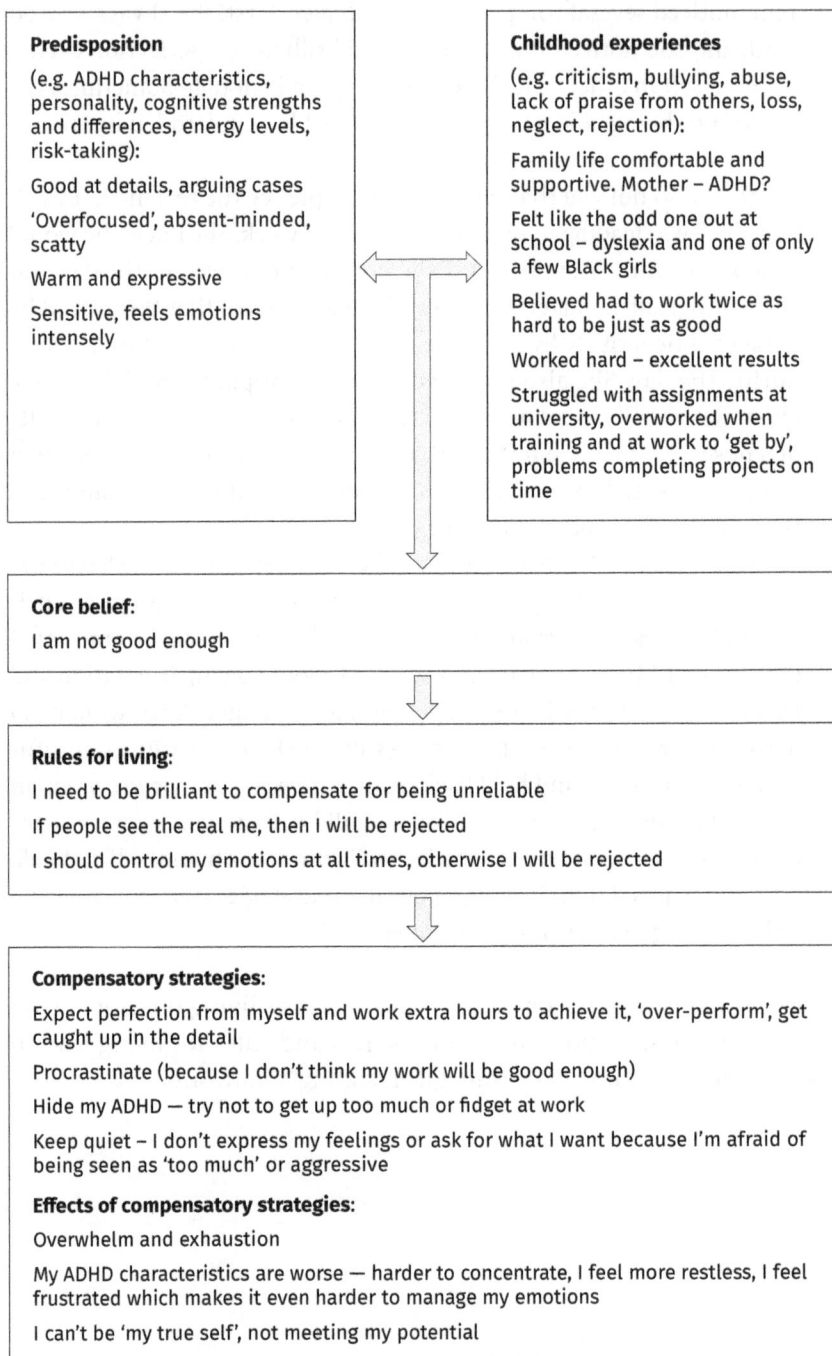

Image A14: *Yemi's core beliefs, rules for living and compensatory strategies*

WORKSHEET: IDENTIFYING CORE BELIEFS AND RULES FOR LIVING

Your therapist will help you to do this using the worksheets in this handout. It is usually best to start with rules for living, as these tend to be a bit easier to identify and change, and then move on to core beliefs when you feel ready.

Identifying your core belief

What do you tell yourself when you are feeling frustrated, upset or down?

....

....

....

Are there any difficult or challenging experiences in your life that stand out?

....

....

....

What did you believe that these meant about you at the time?

....

....

....

If you could sum up any doubts about yourself, what would these be?

....

....

....

Identifying your rules for living

What do you need to do to feel OK as a person and to feel accept-able to others?

Rules may be to do with work, academic achievement, how you look or how you behave with other people. If the rule is inflexible and unreasonable, the chances are it is undermining your self-esteem.

. . . .

. . . .

. . . .

Here are some helpful questions to ask when changing your rules for living.

Where did this rule come from?

. . . .

. . . .

. . . .

Is the rule reasonable (i.e. does it require excessive effort to meet it)?

. . . .

. . . .

. . . .

What are the advantages of the rule?

. . . .

. . . .

. . . .

But what are the disadvantages? What unhelpful coping (compen-satory strategies) does it lead to?

. . . .

. . . .

. . . .

Predisposition

(e.g. ADHD characteristics, personality, cognitive strengths and differences, energy levels, risk-taking):

Childhood experiences

(e.g. criticism, bullying, abuse, lack of praise from others, loss, neglect, rejection):

Core belief:

Rules for living:

Compensatory strategies:

Effects of compensatory strategies:

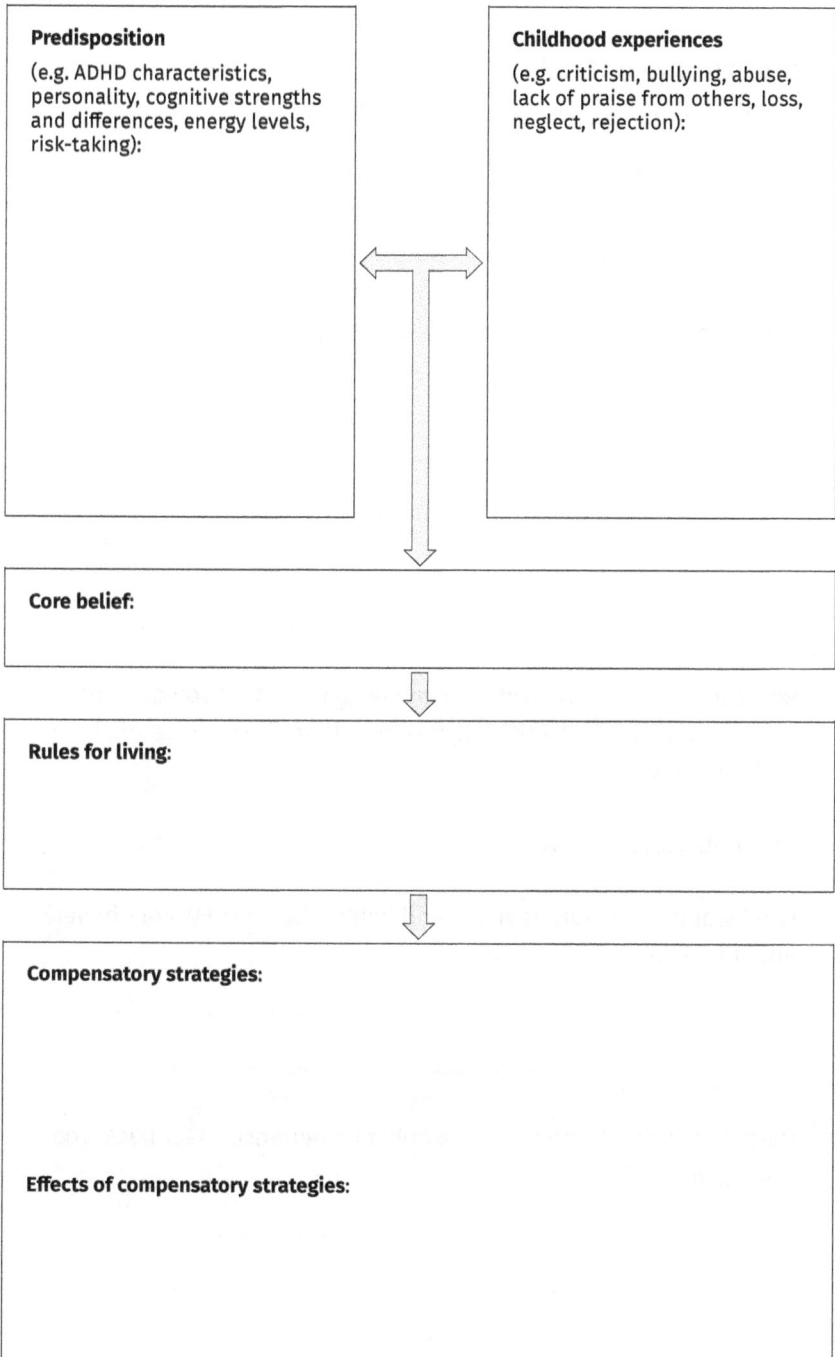

Image A15: My beliefs and coping

Identifying a NEW core belief

What are your good points and qualities?

....

....

What skills do you have? What do you think are the advantages of your ADHD? What do you like about having ADHD?

....

....

What would those who love you say about you?

....

....

Sometimes it helps to identify negative qualities that you don't have, for example 'I am not spiteful', and from that, the positive qualities that must follow.

I am not: ....

What would be a more realistic and helpful belief (NEW core belief) about yourself?

....

....

Data that supports my new core belief (experiences, feedback from others, etc.):

....

....

Identifying NEW rules for living

What would be a more helpful (i.e. flexible) rule that keeps some of the advantages of the old rule but does not have any of the downsides? It is sometimes helpful to think of this as a 'guideline'.

....

....

What can you do to try out this new rule (i.e. how would somebody act who already lived by this rule)?

....

....

Write down what happens when you try it:

....

....

Yemi realized that her differences that had led her to believe she was worse than others were in fact unique and valuable things about herself. For example, she realized that, working in a team, her ability to focus on details was a great strength and complemented the abilities of other team members. In turn, she realized she could ask for help from her manager with the parts of the work that she found more challenging, such as planning her workload.

In her therapy sessions, Yemi explored how her experiences had contributed to her excessively high expectations for herself and her beliefs about others' expectations for her. She thought about how these beliefs had shaped her coping. Yemi reflected that not only had she expected unrealistically high standards for herself, but she had also believed she needed to hide her ADHD challenges as well as her opinions and feelings. Recognizing these beliefs and coping strategies and where they came from helped her find new coping behaviours that were more aligned with her values. These included allowing herself to make mistakes, to seek help and to express her views and emotions. This helped her to feel more confident and content with who she was and how she related to others. Image A16 shows Yemi's new beliefs and coping strategies.

NEW Core belief

I am OK just the way I am; I contribute in unique and valuable ways.

NEW Rules for living

It is good enough for me to be good enough and to do the best I can with the time that I have. I value doing things to a high standard; a high standard is 'nice to have' but I don't have to do everything perfectly.

Not everyone will agree with me or like me. I am allowed to express my views respectfully. I know my heart is in the right place and my family and friends love me.

Having emotions is part of being human and connects me to others — it is good to express my feelings (and acknowledging my feelings helps me be 'assertive' not 'explosive').

NEW (Helpful) coping behaviours

Stick to my work hours: plan my time, break tasks down, take breaks, reward myself during the day, go for walks, stretch.

Seek support and have regular meetings to help me stay on track.

Communicate with work: consider discussing reasonable adjustments with my manager (and sharing my diagnoses). Speak up when my workload is too high.

Be kind to myself when things don't go to plan; try to guide myself gently back on track without telling myself off.

Express how I feel. Write down how I feel or talk to my husband.

Share my opinions.

Ask for help.

Make time to exercise and to do things I enjoy such as spend time with family and friends.

Image A16: Yemi's new beliefs and coping behaviours

You can use Image A17 to note your own new beliefs and coping behaviours.

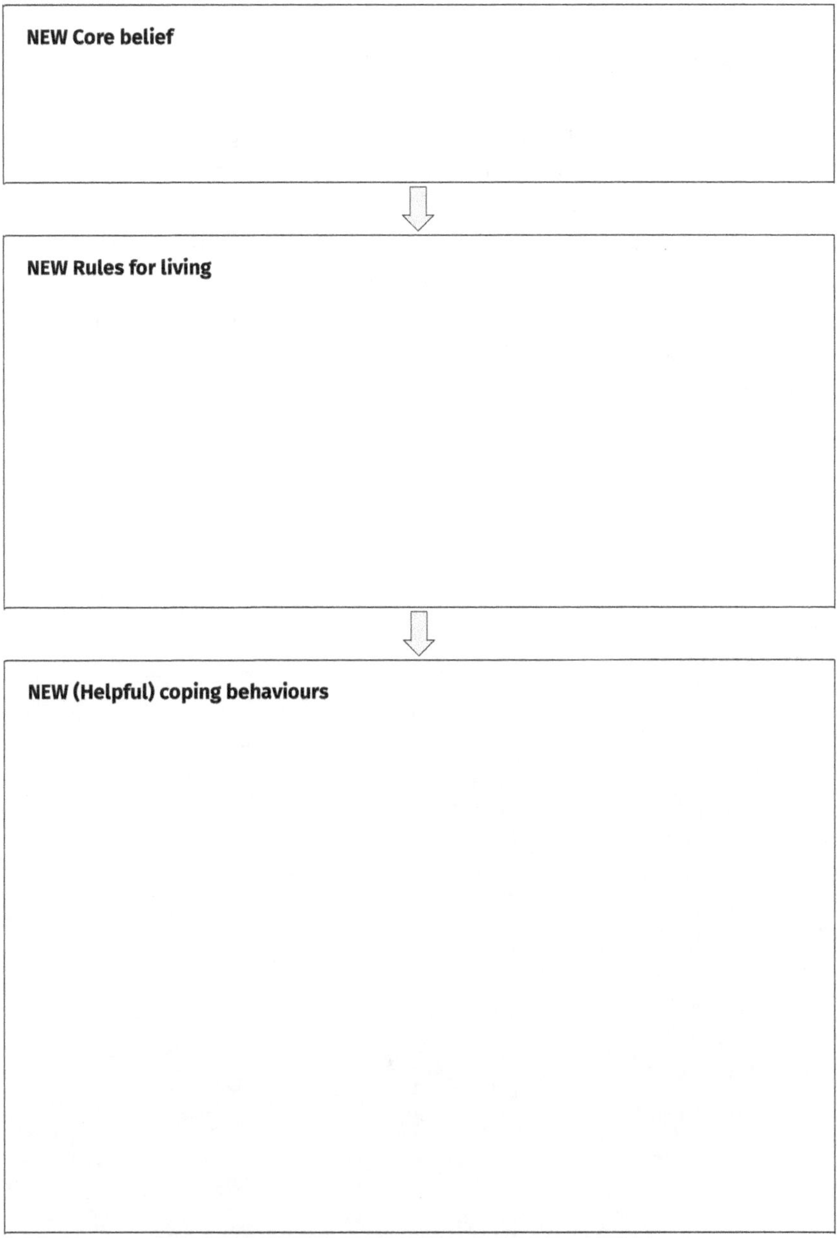

NEW Core belief

⬇

NEW Rules for living

⬇

NEW (Helpful) coping behaviours

Image A17: My new beliefs and coping behaviours

It takes time and practice to develop new beliefs and coping strategies. You can discuss with your therapist ways to test and strengthen your own.

Handout summary

- Core beliefs and rules for living make sense given our experiences; however, they are overgeneralizations and can lead to unhelpful coping behaviours.
- It is possible to adjust core beliefs and rules for living by going through certain steps to challenge them.
- This helps develop new, more helpful coping behaviours and to feel more confident and content.
- It takes time and practice to develop new beliefs and coping behaviours.

SUPPLEMENTARY HANDOUT: PERFECTIONISM

The perfect is the enemy of the good.

VOLTAIRE

Is perfectionism a problem?

'Perfectionism' is the tendency to expect an extremely high or flawless standard of yourself or of others. Trying to do things to high standards is not itself a problem. Indeed, research shows that people who strive towards clear personal goals often feel motivated, achieve the things they want and feel good about themselves. Perfectionism becomes 'unhealthy' when it is applied to too many areas of life, when standards are unrealistically high or rigid or when a person judges their self-worth based on their ability to achieve them.

Perfectionism takes many forms and can affect different areas of life: it may be about work, relationships, appearance, emotions (e.g. a belief that one should not have uncomfortable or distressing emotional experiences) or other things. Perfectionism can feature in ADHD but is also often seen in other conditions. It can make it hard for people to start or complete tasks. Perfectionism may lead people to doubt or question their actions and to become preoccupied with small details or mistakes. It is often associated with low mood and anxiety.

Where does perfectionism come from?

Some people may be predisposed to prefer things to be 'just so', to think in 'all or nothing' terms or to have difficulty tolerating uncertainty. At the same time, perfectionism can be a coping strategy to deal with difficult experiences: some people who develop perfectionism have been criticized and so learned that doing things well helped them avoid unpleasant consequences. Others may have received positive feedback for doing things very well and have come to believe that they need to always keep this up.

Advantages and disadvantages of perfectionism

Many people report being afraid that if they let go of their perfectionism, their standards will slip and they will become a 'second-rate' person. There may be pay-offs for perfectionism such as positive feedback from others. However, perfectionism may be holding them back. It may make them critical of what they do or prevent them from trying in the first place. Doing things perfectly is an unrealistic standard to live up to. It is not possible to always achieve the highest of standards or get things right. Life is filled with ups and downs: problems and crises occur unexpectedly, and others do not always behave in the way we wish them to.

Do you think you may be a perfectionist? If so, what may have started it off and kept it going?

List the advantages and disadvantages of your perfectionism below:

Advantages	Disadvantages

What would happen if you dropped your perfectionism? Are there thoughts (fears?) about what could happen?

Could there be any advantages?

I am going to drop perfectionism by:

Next step:

Dropping perfectionism

The advantages of dropping perfectionism are taking action (as opposed to overthinking) and therefore getting more done, feeling more confident, developing better relationships and becoming more tolerant of feelings in yourself and others. Overall, you are likely to feel more comfortable in your skin. Feelings of satisfaction tend to flow from the *process* of doing something rather than the goal itself. Many people report that achievements based purely on perfectionist ideals feel 'empty' very quickly. On the other hand, if you approach a task with interest and commitment, you will have a richer experience along the way and the end goal will take care of itself.

Some things to try:

- Choose an activity and then aim to do only 50% or 75% rather than to finish it.
- Limit the amount of time you spend on an activity and stop when the time is up.
- Record the activities that you do and rate how satisfying they were and how perfectly you did them – notice whether the two things were related.
- Look out for specific thoughts related to perfectionism and challenge them (see 'Common thinking patterns in ADHD' in **Core Handout**: CBT and Adult ADHD). Try to notice any biases such as 'all-or-nothing' thinking.
- Devise an experiment where you deliberately try to do something to a less-than-perfect standard and then note the results (i.e. do others really respond as negatively as you predict? Are there any unexpected positive outcomes?).

CORE HANDOUT: ENDING THERAPY AND LOOKING AHEAD
Well done!

You have shown courage and determination to get to this point. In this handout, we will be celebrating the changes you have made and helping you think ahead so that you can keep doing what is working for you so far and continue to work towards your goals.

Reviewing progress so far

Look back to **Core Handout**: CBT and Adult ADHD and the goals that you set then. Use the spaces below to write out the goals and then circle the new number that reflects how often you can do it now.

WORKSHEET: RE-RATING THERAPY GOALS

Session number: ....

Date: ....

Things I wanted to be able to do by the end of CBT:

I. ....

   I can now do this:

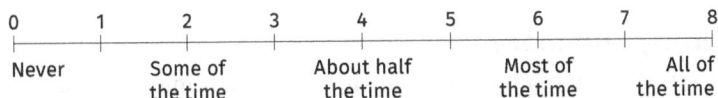

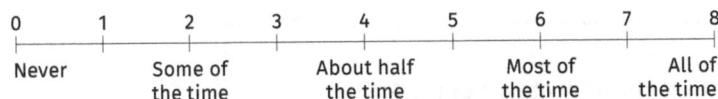

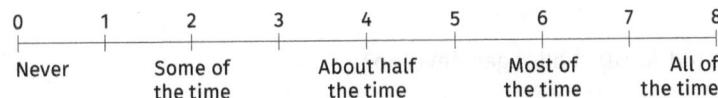

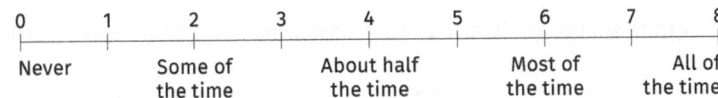

0	1	2	3	4	5	6	7	8
Never		Some of the time		About half the time		Most of the time		All of the time

2. ....

   I can now do this:

0	1	2	3	4	5	6	7	8
Never		Some of the time		About half the time		Most of the time		All of the time

3. ....

   I can now do this:

0	1	2	3	4	5	6	7	8
Never		Some of the time		About half the time		Most of the time		All of the time

4. ....

   I can now do this:

0	1	2	3	4	5	6	7	8
Never		Some of the time		About half the time		Most of the time		All of the time

How does it feel to look over the new ratings? Take a few moments to acknowledge the efforts you have made to get to this point! Try to notice what has gone well, either in changes you have made or the way you have approached things. Can you think of an end-of-therapy reward to celebrate?

Are some ratings lower than you would like? What may be the reasons for this? Watch out for any unrealistic standards or self-criticism. Are there things you can do or continue to work on to bring the ratings closer to where you would like them? The Therapy Summary below may help you answer these questions.

Therapy Summary

What challenges related to my ADHD have I identified? (E.g. disorganization, low self-esteem)

. . . .

. . . .

. . . .

What are the advantages of my ADHD?

. . . .

. . . .

. . . .

How did ADHD challenges develop?

. . . .

. . . .

. . . .

What kept them going? (E.g. avoiding activities, trying to do too much)

. . . .

. . . .

. . . .

What strategies have been helpful while addressing these challenges during CBT? What have I learned? (E.g. identifying thoughts, using a diary, self-compassion)

....
....
....

What areas would I still like to work on?

....
....
....

What are the warning signs that my challenges may be getting worse again?

....
....
....

If I notice challenges getting worse again, what can I do to make things better?

....
....
....

Targets for the next three months:

....
....
....

Blank Therapy Forms to be Used as Needed

Therapy Record Form

Activity Diary

Thought Record

Emotion Diary

Following and Resisting the Impulse

Impulse Log

Anger Log

Worksheet: Re-Rating Therapy Goals

Therapy Record Form

Session number: ....   Date: ....

Before the next session I will work on the following therapy goal(s):

....

The next step(s) is/are:

....

Write these targets in the space below and mark in the box every day that you manage them:

Targets	Mon	Tue	Wed	Thurs	Fri	Sat	Sun	Mon	Tue	Wed	Thurs	Fri	Sat	Sun
....														
....														
....														

Before the next session I will also:

....

....

....

....

Rewards and enjoyable activities (what and when):

....

....

....

Next session date: ....

Next session I would like to talk about:

....

....

....

Activity Diary

Week commencing:	Monday	Tuesday	Wednesday	Thursday	Friday	Saturday	Sunday
Hours asleep last night							
6am–8am							
8am–10am							
10am–12pm							
12pm–2pm							
2pm–4pm							

4pm–6pm						
6pm–8pm						
8pm–10pm						
10pm–midnight						
Midnight–6am						
Time I went to sleep						

Thought Record

Complete this as soon as possible after you notice a change in how you are feeling.

Situation	Thought	Emotion	Physical	Behaviour	Consequence?
	What went through your mind? Rate belief in 'hot' thought (0–100%) Can you spot any thinking biases?	What emotions were around? Rate emotion (0–100%)	What did you feel in your body? Rate intensity (0–100%)	What did you do/ what do you want to do?	What happened?

↑

Re-frame

	Thought	Emotion	Physical	Behaviour
	Alternative thought	What emotions are around now? Re-rate emotion (0–100%)	What can you feel in your body now? Rate intensity (0–100%)	What can you do now?

Emotion Diary

Date and situation	What is the name of the emotion(s) or feeling(s)? Rate intensity (0–100%)	What can you feel in your body?	Are there any thoughts going through your mind about this emotion?	What does this emotion make you want to do? (What is the impulse?)	What happens if you stop and stay with this experience? Make a note of any observations Re-rate emotional intensity

FOLLOWING AND RESISTING THE IMPULSE

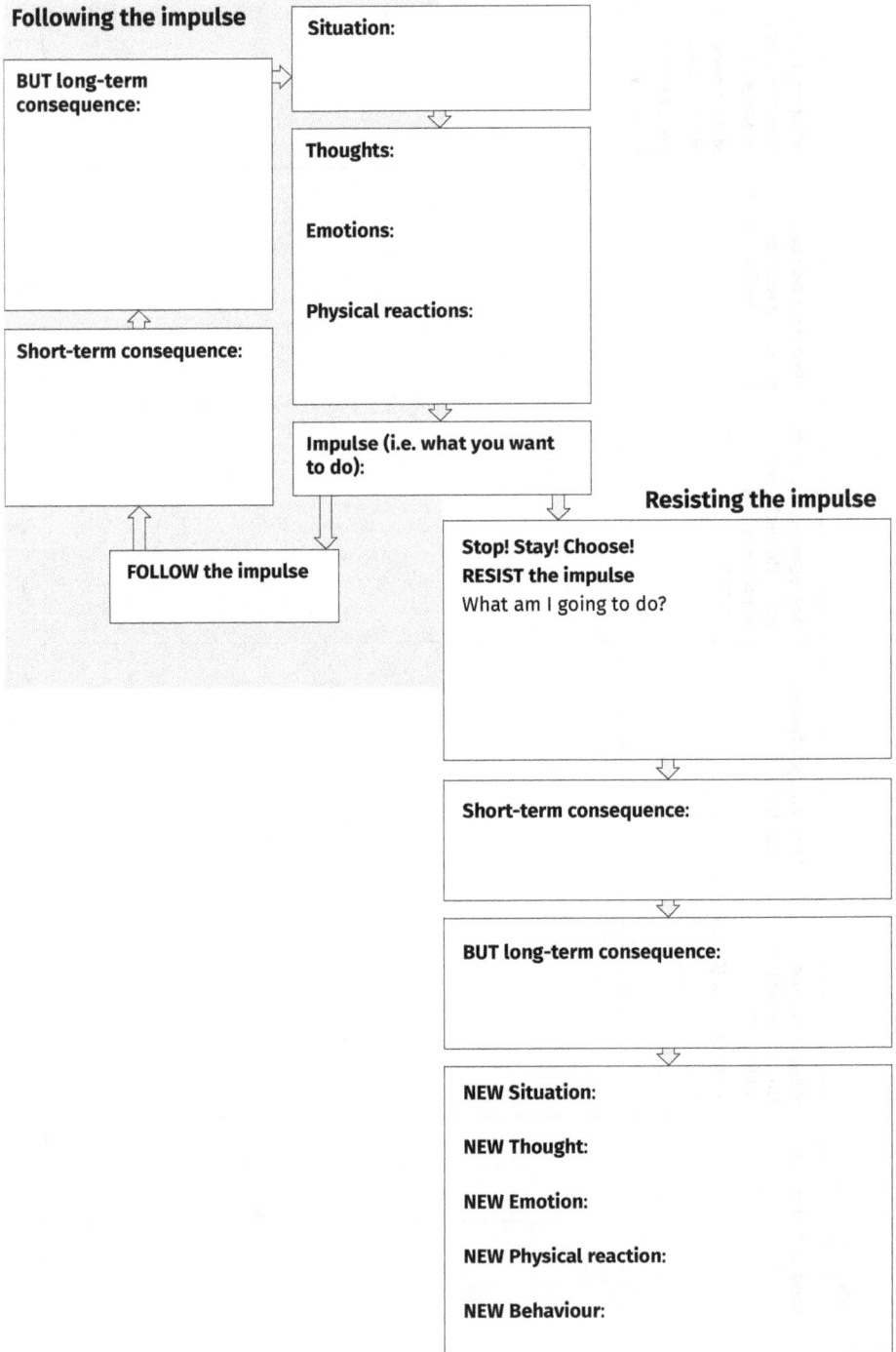

Following the impulse

Situation:

BUT long-term consequence:

Thoughts:

Emotions:

Physical reactions:

Short-term consequence:

Impulse (i.e. what you want to do):

Resisting the impulse

FOLLOW the impulse

Stop! Stay! Choose!
RESIST the impulse
What am I going to do?

Short-term consequence:

BUT long-term consequence:

NEW Situation:

NEW Thought:

NEW Emotion:

NEW Physical reaction:

NEW Behaviour:

Impulse Log

Situation Date, time, what were you doing?	Impulse (What did you feel like doing?)	Thoughts What went through your mind?	Emotions Rate intensity (0-100%)	Physical sensations (feelings in your body)	Stop! Stay! Choose! What did you think or say to yourself? What did you do?	What happened at first? What thoughts, emotions (rate 0-100%), physical sensations were there at first? (Short-term consequence)	Outcome What happened next? What thoughts, emotions (rate 0-100%), physical sensations followed? (Long-term consequence)

Anger Log

Trigger What happened? Who was there, what was said and done?	Thoughts What went through your mind? What did the situation mean to you?	Emotion How intense was it? (0–100%)	Physical sensations	Your response What did you say/do?	Short-term consequence	Long-term consequence	Was there an alternative, more helpful response? Is there anything you could have said / done instead?

WORKSHEET: RE-RATING THERAPY GOALS

Session number: ....

Date: ....

Things I wanted to be able to do by the end of CBT:

I. ....

    I can now do this:

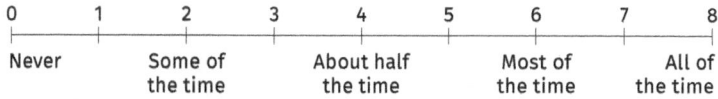

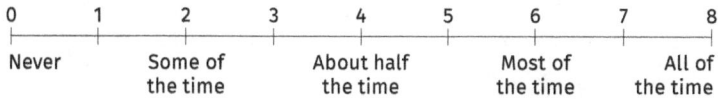

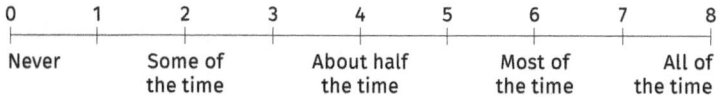

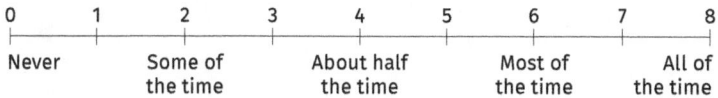

0	1	2	3	4	5	6	7	8
Never		Some of the time		About half the time		Most of the time		All of the time

2. ....

    I can now do this:

0	1	2	3	4	5	6	7	8
Never		Some of the time		About half the time		Most of the time		All of the time

3. ....

    I can now do this:

0	1	2	3	4	5	6	7	8
Never		Some of the time		About half the time		Most of the time		All of the time

4. ....

    I can now do this:

0	1	2	3	4	5	6	7	8
Never		Some of the time		About half the time		Most of the time		All of the time

References

Attoe, D. E. and Climie, E. A. (2023) 'Miss. Diagnosis: A systematic review of ADHD in adult women.' *Journal of Attention Disorders* [online] *27*, 7 10870547231615.

Banerjee, T., Bari, M., Yemula, C., Ajmal, S., Khan, A. and Arora, R. (2024) '6313 Ethnic diversity of children and young people with attention deficit hyperactivity disorder: Observation from a single centre.' *Archives of Disease in Childhood 109*, A270–A271.

Beaton, D. M., Sirois, F. and Milne, E. (2020) 'Self-compassion and perceived criticism in adults with attention deficit hyperactivity disorder (ADHD).' *Mindfulness 11*, 2506–2518.

Beck, A. T., Rush, A. J., Shaw, B. F. and Emery, G. (1979) *Cognitive Therapy of Depression.* New York: Guilford Press.

Beck, J. S. (2020) *Cognitive Behavior Therapy: Basics and Beyond.* 3rd ed. New York: Guilford Press.

Björkenstam, E., Björkenstam, C., Jablonska, B. and Kosidou, K. (2017) 'Cumulative exposure to childhood adversity, and treated attention deficit/hyperactivity disorder: A cohort study of 543 650 adolescents and young adults in Sweden.' *Psychological Medicine 48*, 3, 498–507.

Blackburn, I.-M., James, I. A., Milne, D. L., Baker, C., Standart, S., Garland, A. and Reichelt, F. K. (2001) 'The Revised Cognitive Therapy Scale (CTS-R): Psychometric properties.' *Behavioural and Cognitive Psychotherapy 29*, 4, 431–446.

Cherkasova, M. V., French, L. R., Syer, C. A., Cousins, L., Galina, H., Ahmadi-Kashani, Y. and Hechtman, L. (2016) 'Efficacy of cognitive behavioral therapy with and without medication for adults with ADHD.' *Journal of Attention Disorders 24*, 6, 10870547166719.

Dittner, A. J., Hodsoll, J., Rimes, K. A., Russell, A. J. and Chalder, T. (2018) 'Cognitive-behavioural therapy for adult attention-deficit hyperactivity disorder: A proof of concept randomised controlled trial.' *Acta Psychiatrica Scandinavica 137*, 2, 125–137.

Dittner, A. J., Rimes, K. A., Russell, A. J. and Chalder, T. (2014) 'Protocol for a proof of concept randomized controlled trial of cognitive-behavioural therapy for adult ADHD as a supplement to treatment as usual, compared with treatment as usual alone.' *BMC Psychiatry 14*, 1.

Dobson, K. S. and Kazantzis, N. (2023) 'Therapeutic relationships in cognitive behavioral therapy: Tailoring the therapeutic alliance.' *Psychotherapy Research 33*, 1, 1–2.

Equality Act 2010. www.legislation.gov.uk/ukpga/2010/15/contents.

Fadus, M. C., Ginsburg, K. R., Sobowale, K., Halliday-Boykins, C. A., Bryant, B. E., Gray, K. M. and Squeglia, L. M. (2020) 'Unconscious bias and the diagnosis of disruptive behavior disorders and ADHD in African American and Hispanic Youth.' *Academic Psychiatry* [online] *44*, 1, 95–102.

Faraone, S. V., Asherson, P., Banaschewski, T., Biederman, J., Buitelaar, J. K., Ramos-Quiroga, J. A., Rohde, L. A., Sonuga-Barke, E. J. S., Tannock, R. and Franke, B. (2015) 'Attention-deficit/hyperactivity disorder.' *Nature Reviews Disease Primers* [online] *1*, 15020.

Faugno, E., Galbraith, A. A., Walsh, K., Maglione, P. J., Farmer, J. R. and Ong, M.-S. (2024) 'Experiences with diagnostic delay among underserved racial and ethnic patients: A systematic review of the qualitative literature.' *BMJ Quality & Safety* [online] *34*, 3, 190–200.

Fennell, M. J. V. (2016) *Overcoming Low Self-Esteem: A Self-Help Guide Using Cognitive Behavioral Techniques.* London: Robinson.

Fullen, T., Jones, S. L., Emerson, L. M. and Adamou, M. (2020) 'Psychological treatments in adult ADHD: A systematic review.' *Journal of Psychopathology and Behavioral Assessment* 42, 3, 500–518.

Gilbert, P. (2010) *Compassion Focused Therapy: Distinctive Features.* London: Routledge.

Harpin, V., Mazzone, L., Raynaud, J. P., Kahle, J. and Hodgkins, P. (2016) 'Long-term outcomes of ADHD: A systematic review of self-esteem and social function.' *Journal of Attention Disorders* [online] *20*, 4, 295–305.

Katzman, M. A., Bilkey, T. S., Chokka, P. R., Fallu, A. and Klassen, L. J. (2017) 'Adult ADHD and comorbid disorders: Clinical implications of a dimensional approach.' *BMC Psychiatry* [online] *17*, 1.

Kazantzis, N., Dattilio, F. M. and Dobson, K. S. (2017) *The Therapeutic Relationship in Cognitive-Behavioral Therapy: A Clinician's Guide.* New York: Guilford Press.

Lakein, A. (1973) *How to Get Control of Your Time and Your Life.* New York: Signet.

Linehan, M. (1993) *Cognitive-Behavioral Treatment of Borderline Personality Disorder.* New York: Guilford Press.

Liu, C.-I., Hua, M.-H., Lu, M.-L. and Goh, K. K. (2023) 'Effectiveness of cognitive behavioural-based interventions for adults with attention-deficit/hyperactivity disorder extends beyond core symptoms: A meta-analysis of randomized controlled trials.' *Psychology and Psychotherapy* [online] *96*, 3, 543–559.

Martin, J. (2024) 'Why are females less likely to be diagnosed with ADHD in childhood than males?' *The Lancet Psychiatry 11*, 4.

McManus, F., Van Doorn, K. and Yiend, J. (2012) 'Examining the effects of Therapy Records and behavioral experiments in instigating belief change.' *Journal of Behavior Therapy and Experimental Psychiatry 43*, 1, 540–547.

Mitchell, J. T., Benson, J. W., Knouse, L. E., Kimbrel, N. A. and Anastopoulos, A. D. (2013) 'Are negative automatic thoughts associated with ADHD in adulthood?' *Cognitive Therapy and Research 37*, 4, 851–859.

Mueller, A. K., Fuermaier, A. B., Koerts, J. and Tucha, L. (2012) 'Stigma in attention deficit hyperactivity disorder.' *Attention Deficit and Hyperactivity Disorders 4*, 3, 101–114.

National Autistic Society (n.d.) How to talk and write about autism. https://dy55nndrxkeɪw.cloudfront.net/file/24/xT2FqU_xTh5_JA5xTMYZxb.dfVox/NAS_How%20to%20talk%20and%20write%20about%20autism.pdf

National Institute for Health and Care Excellence (2018) Attention deficit hyperactivity disorder: Diagnosis and management. www.nice.org.uk/guidance/ng87

Ofori, M. (2024) 'UK's black children "face cultural barriers" in accessing help for autism and ADHD.' *The Guardian* [online], 31 March. www.theguardian.com/education/2024/mar/31/uk-black-children-cultural-barriers-accessing-help-autism-adhd

Padesky, C. A. and Greenberger, D. (1995) *Clinician's Guide to Mind Over Mood*. New York: Guilford Press.

Pan, M.-R., Huang, F., Zhao, M.-J., Wang, Y.-F., Wang, Y.-F. and Qian, Q.-J. (2019) 'A comparison of efficacy between cognitive behavioral therapy (CBT) and CBT combined with medication in adults with attention-deficit/hyperactivity disorder (ADHD).' *Psychiatry Research 279*, 23–33.

Plutchik, R. (2001) 'The nature of emotions: Human emotions have deep evolutionary roots, a fact that may explain their complexity and provide tools for clinical practice.' *American Scientist 89*, 4, 344–350.

Polanczyk, G. V., Willcutt, E. G., Salum, G. A., Kieling, C. and Rohde, L. A. (2014) 'ADHD prevalence estimates across three decades: An updated systematic review and meta-regression analysis.' *International Journal of Epidemiology* [online] *43*, 2, 434–442.

Ramsay, J. R. and Rostain, A. L. (2014) *Cognitive-Behavioral Therapy for Adult ADHD: An Integrative Psychosocial and Medical Approach*. New York: Routledge, Taylor and Francis.

Redhead, S., Johnstone, L. and Nightingale, J. (2015) 'Clients' experiences of formulation in cognitive behaviour therapy.' *Psychology and Psychotherapy: Theory, Research and Practice* [online] *88*, 4, 453–467.

Rincón, C. F., Morales, L. B. and Sandoval, S. T. (2024) 'Executive functioning in adults with attention deficit hyperactivity disorder: A systematic review.' *Acta Neurológica Colombiana 40*, 3.

Safren, S. A., Sprich, S. E., Perlman, C. A. and Otto, M. W. (2017) *Mastering Your Adult ADHD*. New York: Oxford University Press.

Schein, J., Childress, A., Cloutier, M., Desai, U., Chin, A., Simes, M., Guerin, A. and Adams, J. (2022) 'Reasons for treatment changes in adults with attention-deficit/hyperactivity disorder: A chart review study.' *BMC Psychiatry* [online] *22*, 1, 377.

Segal, Z. V., Williams, J. M., Teasdale, J. D. and Kabat-Zinn, J. (2012) *Mindfulness-Based Cognitive Therapy for Depression* (2nd ed.). New York: Guilford Press.

Siegel, D. J. (1999) *The Developing Mind: Toward a Neurobiology of Interpersonal Experience*. New York: Guilford Press.

Siegel, D. J. (2024) *Window of Tolerance Card*. Norton Professional Books.

Shafran, R., Egan, S. and Wade, T. (2018) *Overcoming Perfectionism*. London: Robinson.

Shi, Y., Hunter Guevara, L. R., Dykhoff, H. J., Sangaralingham, L. R., Phelan, S., Zaccariello, M. J. and Warner, D. O. (2021) 'Racial disparities in diagnosis of attention-deficit/hyperactivity disorder in a US national birth cohort.' *JAMA Network Open 4*, 3.

Shim, S.-H., Yoon, H., Bak, J., Hahn, S.-W. and Kim, Y.-K. (2016) 'Clinical and neurobiological factors in the management of treatment refractory attention-deficit hyperactivity disorder.' *Progress in Neuro-Psychopharmacology and Biological Psychiatry 70*, 237–244.

Slobodin, O. and Masalha, R. (2020) 'Challenges in ADHD care for ethnic minority children: A review of the current literature.' *Transcultural Psychiatry 57*, 3, 468–483.

Song, P., Zha, M., Yang, Q., Zhang, Y., Li, X. and Rudan, I. (2021) 'The prevalence of adult attention-deficit hyperactivity disorder: A global systematic review and meta-analysis.' *Journal of Global Health 11*, 04009.

Steel, P. (2007) 'The nature of procrastination: A meta-analytic and theoretical review of quintessential self-regulatory failure.' *Psychological Bulletin* [online] *133*, 1, 65–94.

Strohmeier, C. W., Rosenfield, B., DiTomasso, R. A. and Ramsay, J. R. (2016) 'Assessment of the relationship between self-reported cognitive distortions and adult ADHD, anxiety, depression, and hopelessness.' *Psychiatry Research 238*, 153–158.

Van der Weel, F. R. R. and Van der Meer, A. L. H. (2024) 'Handwriting but not type-writing leads to widespread brain connectivity: A high-density EEG study with implications for the classroom.' *Frontiers in Psychology 14*, 14.

Warrier, V., Greenberg, D. M., Weir, E., Buckingham, C., Smith, P., Lai, M.-C., Allison, C. and Baron-Cohen, S. (2020) 'Elevated rates of autism, other neurodevelopmental and psychiatric diagnoses, and autistic traits in transgender and gender-diverse individuals.' *Nature Communications* [online] *11*, 1.

Weiss, M., Murray, C., Wasdell, M., Greenfield, B., Giles, L. and Hechtman, L. (2012) 'A randomized controlled trial of CBT therapy for adults with ADHD with and without medication.' *BMC Psychiatry 12*, 1.

Willcox, G. (1982) 'The Feeling Wheel.' *Transactional Analysis Journal 12*, 4, 274–276.

Winter, S., Diamond, M., Green, J., Karasic, D., Reed, T., Whittle, S. and Wylie, K. (2016) 'Transgender people: Health at the margins of society.' *The Lancet 388*, 10042, 390–400.

Young, S. and Bramham, J. (2006) *ADHD in Adults: A Psychological Guide to Practice*. Chichester: John Wiley & Sons.

Subject Index

233

Author Index

RAISING READERS
Books Build Bright Futures

Dear Reader,

We'd love your attention for one more page to tell you about the crisis in children's reading, and what we can all do.

Studies have shown that reading for fun is the **single biggest predictor of a child's future life chances** – more than family circumstance, parents' educational background or income. It improves academic results, mental health, wealth, communication skills, ambition and happiness.[1]

The number of children reading for fun is in rapid decline. Young people have a lot of competition for their time. In 2024, 1 in 10 children and young people in the UK aged 5 to 18 did not own a single book at home.[2]

Hachette works extensively with schools, libraries and literacy charities, but here are some ways we can all raise more readers:

- Reading to children for just 10 minutes a day makes a difference
- Don't give up if children aren't regular readers – there will be books for them!
- Visit bookshops and libraries to get recommendations
- Encourage them to listen to audiobooks
- Support school libraries
- Give books as gifts

There's a lot more information about how to encourage children to read on our website: **www.RaisingReaders.co.uk**

Thank you for reading.

hachette
UK

---

1   OECD, '21st-Century Readers: Developing Literacy Skills in a Digital World', 2021, https://www.oecd.org/en/publications/21st-century-readers_a83d84cb-en.html
2   National Literacy Trust, 'Book Ownership in 2024', November 2024, https://literacytrust.org.uk/research-services/research-reports/book-ownership-in-2024